CRAFTING CAPTAINS

The Handbook of Leadership Excellence

Mohammed Mahmoud El-Arabi

Copyright © 2023 byMohammed Mahmoud El-Arabi
All rights reserved.

Table of Contents

1. Overview of the Handbook 1
   1.1. What Is Executive Coaching? 2
   1.2. Why Executive Coaching Is Important 3
   1.3. Can Coaching Make Great Leaders? 4

2.1. Fundamental Areas of Focus 7

Chapter One: 3. Leadership 9
   3.1. Who Is a Leader? 9
   3.2. Key Areas of Focus for Leadership 10
      3.2.1. Advanced Communication 11
         3.2.1.1. Active Listening 12
         3.2.1.1.1. How to Become an Active Listener *13*
         3.2.1.2. Interaction 14
         3.2.1.2.1. How to Improve Interactions *15*
         3.2.1.3. Empathy 16
         3.2.1.3.1. How to Improve Empathy *17*
         3.2.1.4. Pitching 18
         3.2.1.4.1. How to Improve Pitching *20*
         3.2.1.5. Building Trust 21
         3.2.1.5.1. How to Improve on Building Trust *22*
         3.2.1.6. Open-Door Policy 23
         3.2.1.6.1. How to Improve the Effectiveness of Your Organization's Open-Door Policy *24*
         3.2.1.7. Transparency 25
         3.2.1.7.1. How to Improve Transparency *26*
      3.2.2. Effective Skills 28
         3.2.2.1. Influencing 28
         3.2.2.1.1. How to Improve Your Influencing Skills *30*
         3.2.2.2. Motivation 31
         3.2.2.2.1. How to Improve Your Motivation Skills *32*
         3.2.2.3. Negotiation 33
         3.2.2.3.1. How to Improve Your Negotiation Skills *34*
         3.2.2.4. Creativity 35
         3.2.2.4.1. How to Improve Your Creativity Skills *36*

Table of Contents

- 3.2.2.5. Relationship Building 37
  - *3.2.2.5.1. How to Improve Your Relationship Building Skills* *38*
- 3.2.2.6. Mentoring 39
  - *3.2.2.6.1. How to Improve Your Mentoring Skills* *40*
- 3.2.3. Awareness 41
  - 3.2.3.1. Bottlenecks and Roadblocks 42
    - *3.2.3.1.1. How to Improve Your Awareness of Bottlenecks and Roadblocks* *43*
  - 3.2.3.2. Organizational Strategy and Goals 44
    - *3.2.3.2.1. How to Improve Your Awareness of Organizational Strategy and Goals* *45*
  - 3.2.3.3. Organizational Policy and Procedures 46
    - *3.2.3.3.1. How to Improve Your Awareness of Organizational Policy and Procedures* *47*
  - 3.2.3.4. Employee Strengths and Weaknesses 48
    - *3.2.3.4.1. How to Improve Your Awareness of Employee Strengths and Weaknesses* *49*
  - 3.2.3.5. Organizational Communication Guidelines 50
    - *3.2.3.5.1. How to Improve Your Awareness of Organizational Communication Guidelines* *51*
  - 3.2.3.6. Latest Trends 52
    - *3.2.3.6.1. How to Improve Your Awareness of the Latest Trends* *53*
- 3.2.4. Delegation 54
  - 3.2.4.1. R & R Matrix 54
    - *3.2.4.1.1. How to Improve on the R&R Matrix* *58*
  - 3.2.4.2. Knowing Your Team 59
    - *3.2.4.2.1. How to Improve on Knowing Your Team* *60*
  - 3.2.4.3. Setting Expectations 61
    - *3.2.4.3.1. How to Improve on Setting Expectations* *64*
  - 3.2.4.4. Empowering the Team 65
    - *3.2.4.4.1. How to Improve on Empowering the Team* *67*
  - 3.2.4.5. Motivation and Recognition 68
    - *3.2.4.5.1. How to Improve Motivation and Recognition* *70*
  - 3.2.4.6. Respect and Integrity 71
    - *3.2.4.6.1. How to Improve Respect and Integrity* *73*
  - 3.2.4.7. Avoiding Micromanagement 74
    - *3.2.4.7.1. How to Improve on Avoiding Micromanagement* *75*

Chapter Two: 4. Operations 77

- 4.1. What Is Operations 77
- 4.2. Key Areas of Focus for Operations 78
  - 4.2.1. Improve Productivity 78
    - 4.2.1.1. Communication Gaps 78
      - *4.2.1.1.1. How to Minimize Communication Gaps* *80*
    - 4.2.1.2. Roadblocks 81
      - *4.2.1.2.1. How to Minimize Roadblocks* *82*
    - 4.2.1.3. Realistic Goals 83
      - *4.2.1.3.1. How to Improve on Setting Realistic Goal* *84*

Table of Contents

- 4.2.1.4. Skills Gaps 85
  - *4.2.1.4.1. How to Minimize Skill Gaps* *86*
- 4.2.1.5. Reduce Distractions 87
  - *4.2.1.5.1. How to Reduce Distractions* *88*
- 4.2.1.6. Positive Reinforcement and Team Building 89
  - *4.2.1.6.1. How to Improve on Positive Reinforcement* *89*
- 4.2.1.7. Improving Workplace Conditions 90
- 4.2.2. Stabilize Performance 91
  - 4.2.2.1. Stabilize Challenges 91
    - *4.2.2.1.1. How to Improve Stabilizing Challenges* *92*
  - 4.2.2.2. Synchronization and Collaboration Challenges 93
    - *4.2.2.2.1. How to Minimize Synchronization and Collaboration Challenges* *94*
  - 4.2.2.3. Operational Benchmarking & Excellence 95
  - 4.2.2.4. Current vs To-be Gaps 96
    - *4.2.2.4.1. How to Manage Current vs To-be Gaps* *96*
  - 4.2.2.5. Set up KPIs 97
    - *4.2.2.5.1. How to Improve on Setting up KPIs* *98*
  - 4.2.2.6. Sustainable Benchmarking 99
    - *4.2.2.6.1. How to Improve on Sustainable Benchmarking* *100*
- 4.2.3. Maturity 101
  - 4.2.3.1. Challenges on Team Alignment and Collaboration 101
    - *4.2.3.1.1. How to Address Challenges on Team Alignment and Collaboration* *101*
  - 4.2.3.2. Lessons Learned 102
    - *4.2.3.2.1. How to Apply Lessons Learned* *103*
  - 4.2.3.3. Revisiting the Business Model and Value Chains 104
    - *4.2.3.3.1. How to Improve on Revisiting the Business Model and Value Chains* *105*
  - 4.2.3.4. Out of the Box Thinking 106
    - *4.2.3.4.1. How to Improve on Out of the Box Thinking* *107*
  - 4.2.3.5. Challenging the Status Quo 108
    - *4.2.3.5.1. How to Improve on Challenging the Status Quo* *109*
  - 4.2.3.6. Continuous Innovation 110
    - *4.2.3.6.1. How to Improve on Continuous Innovation* *111*
- 4.2.4. A Service-Oriented Approach 112
  - 4.2.4.1. Optimum Customer Satisfaction 112
    - *4.2.4.1.1. How to Improve Optimum Customer Satisfaction* *113*
  - 4.2.4.2. Service Levels 114
    - *4.2.4.2.1. How to Improve Service Levels* *115*
  - 4.2.4.3. Root Cause Resolutions 116
    - *4.2.4.3.1. How to Improve on Root Cause Resolutions* *117*
  - 4.2.4.4. Customer Feedback 118
    - *4.2.4.4.1. How to Improve on Customer Feedback* *120*
  - 4.2.4.5. Revisiting Service Levels 121
    - *4.2.4.5.1. How to Improve on Revisiting Service Levels* *122*
  - 4.2.4.6. Revisiting Benchmarks and KPIs 123
    - *4.2.4.6.1. How to Improve on Revisiting Benchmarks and KPIs* *124*
- 4.2.5. Process Improvements 125
  - 4.2.5.1. Process Bottlenecks 125

Table of Contents

    4.2.5.1.1. *How to Minimize Process Bottlenecks* 126
   4.2.5.2. Removal of Non-value adding activities 127
   4.2.5.2.1. *How to Minimize Process Bottlenecks* 128
   4.2.5.3. Adopting Automation 129
   4.2.5.3.1. *How to Improve on Adopting Automation* 130
   4.2.5.4. Continuous Improvement 131
   4.2.5.4.1. *How to Work on Continuous Improvement* 131
  4.2.6. Cost Effectiveness 132
   4.2.6.1. Categorization of Costs 132
   4.2.6.1.1. *How to Improve on Categorization of Costs* 133
   4.2.6.2. Identifying True Costs 134
   4.2.6.2.1. *How to Improve on Identifying True Costs* 135
   4.2.6.3. Consolidation of the Operations 136
   4.2.6.3.1. *How to Improve on Consolidation of Operations* 137
   4.2.6.4. Return on Investment 138
   4.2.6.4.1. *How to Improve on the Return on Investment* 139
   4.2.6.5. Reusability 140
   4.2.6.5.1. *How to Improve on Reusability* 141
   4.2.6.6. Cloud Adoption 142
   4.2.6.6.1. *How to Improve on Cloud Adoption* 143
   4.2.6.7. Going Paperless 144
   4.2.6.7.1. *How to Improve on Going Paperless* 145
   4.2.6.8. Remote Work Culture 146
   4.2.6.8.1. *How to Improve on Remote Work Culture* 147
   4.2.6.9. Sustainable Energy 148
   4.2.6.9.1. *How to Improve on Sustainable Energy* 149
   4.2.6.10. Setting KPIs Around Cost-Cutting 150
   4.2.6.10.1. *How to Improve on Setting KPIs Around Cost-Cutting* 151

Chapter Three: 5. Team 153
5.1. What Is a Team 153
5.2. Key Areas of Focus for a Team 154
 5.2.1. Motivation 154
  5.2.1.1. Awareness of Organization Goals & Targets 154
  5.2.1.1.1. *How to Improve Awareness on Organization Goals and Targets* 156
  5.2.1.2. Delegation of Tasks 157
  5.2.1.2.1. *How to Improve on Delegation of Tasks* 158
  5.2.1.3. Showing Respect 159
  5.2.1.3.1. *How to Improve on Showing Respect* 160
  5.2.1.4. Positive Communication 161
  5.2.1.4.1. *How to Improve on Positive Communication* 162
  5.2.1.5. Positive Competition 163
  5.2.1.5.1. *How to Improve on Positive Competition* 164
  5.2.1.6. Incentives 165
  5.2.1.6.1. *How to Improve on Incentives* 166
  5.2.1.7. Team Outcomes 167
  5.2.1.7.1. *How to Improve on Team Outcomes* 168

Table of Contents

- 5.2.1.8. Flexibility ... 169
  - 5.2.1.8.1. How to Improve on Flexibility ... 170
- 5.2.1.9. Continuous Recognition and Rewarding ... 171
  - 5.2.1.9.1. How to Improve Continuous Recognition and Rewarding ... 172
- 5.2.2. Loyalty ... 173
  - 5.2.2.1. Investing in Employees ... 173
    - 5.2.2.1.1. How to Improve on Investing in Employees ... 174
  - 5.2.2.2. Open-Door Policy ... 175
    - 5.2.2.2.1. How to Improve on an Open-Door Policy ... 176
  - 5.2.2.3. Training and Development ... 177
    - 5.2.2.3.1. How to Improve on Training & Development ... 178
  - 5.2.2.4. Perks and Benefits ... 179
    - 5.2.2.4.1. How to Improve on Perks and Benefits ... 180
  - 5.2.2.5. Extended Focus ... 181
    - 5.2.2.5.1. How to Improve on Extended Focus ... 182
- 5.2.3. Life Balance ... 183
  - 5.2.3.1. Awareness of Work-Life Balance ... 183
    - 5.2.3.1.1. How to Improve Awareness of Work-Life Balance ... 184
  - 5.2.3.2. Effective Usage of Time ... 185
    - 5.2.3.2.1. How to Improve on Effective Usage of Time ... 186
  - 5.2.3.3. Cross-Training ... 187
    - 5.2.3.3.1. How to Improve on Cross Training ... 188
  - 5.2.3.4. Paid Time Off ... 189
    - 5.2.3.4.1. How to Improve on Paid Time Off ... 190
  - 5.2.3.5. Corporate Initiatives ... 191
    - 5.2.3.5.1. How to Improve on Corporate Initiatives ... 192
  - 5.2.3.6. Outcome-Based KPIs ... 193
    - 5.2.3.6.1. How to Improve Outcome-Based KPIs ... 194
  - 5.2.3.7. Flexibility ... 195
- 5.2.4. Strengthening Self-Confidence ... 196
  - 5.2.4.1. Coaching Employees ... 196
    - 5.2.4.1.1. How to Improve on Coaching Employees ... 197
  - 5.2.4.2. Embrace Ideas ... 198
    - 5.2.4.2.1. How to Improve on Embracing Ideas ... 199
  - 5.2.4.3. Showing Respect ... 200
  - 5.2.4.4. Failing Fast ... 201
    - 5.2.4.4.1. How to Fail Fast ... 202
  - 5.2.4.5. Continuous Encouragement ... 203
    - 5.2.4.5.1. How to Improve on Continuous Engagement ... 204
- 5.2.5. Career Development ... 205
  - 5.2.5.1. Setting the Bigger Picture ... 205
    - 5.2.5.1.1. How to Improve on Setting the Big Picture ... 206
  - 5.2.5.2. Career Development Initiatives ... 207
    - 5.2.5.2.1. How to Improve on Career Development Initiatives ... 208
  - 5.2.5.3. Job Shadowing ... 209
    - 5.2.5.3.1. How to Improve on Job Shadowing ... 210

Table of Contents

- 5.2.5.4. Flexibility on Career Path Changes ... 211
  - *5.2.5.4.1. How to Improve on Flexibility on Career Path Changes* ... 212
- 5.2.5.5. Identification of Future Leaders ... 213
  - *5.2.5.5.1. How to Improve on Identification of Future Leaders* ... 214
- 5.2.5.6. Internal Promotions ... 215
  - *5.2.5.6.1. How to Improve on Internal Promotions* ... 216
- 5.2.6. Recognition ... 217
  - 5.2.6.1. Formal and Informal Recognition ... 217
    - *5.2.6.1.1. How to Improve on Formal and Informal Recognitions* ... 218
  - 5.2.6.2. Special Effort Recognition ... 219
    - *5.2.6.2.1. How to Improve on Special Effort Recognition* ... 220
  - 5.2.6.3. Comprehensive Scoring ... 221
    - *5.2.6.3.1. How to Improve on Comprehensive Scoring* ... 222
  - 5.2.6.4. Increasing Employee Visibility ... 223
    - *5.2.6.4.1. How to Improve on Increasing Employee Visibility* ... 224
  - 5.2.6.5. Personal Touch ... 225
    - *5.2.6.5.1. How to Improve on Personal Touch* ... 226
  - 5.2.6.6. Budget Allocations ... 227
    - *5.2.6.6.1. How to Improve on Budget Allocations* ... 228

Purpose of this Handbook

There is a famous Vince Lombardi **quote** that may be familiar to many of you: **Leaders** are **made**, they are **not born**." This self-explanatory quote goes on to say, "They are made by hard effort, which is the price which all of us must pay to achieve any goal that is worthwhile."

Part of that "hard effort" is the ability to make the right decision, especially during turbulent times. This is the kind of leader that all organizations are searching for.

Executive coaching has become one of the most desired areas of focus for many organizations in recent times due to its ability to help build creative, successful leaders. Coaching and mentoring are ways of guiding and molding individuals in a structured way, grooming them into successful leaders. Its impact is not just on the development of the individuals but also consequently on the organization, enabling it to navigate the complexities of transition and change.

The purpose of this handbook is to provide comprehensive coaching to **executives** to help their leaders transform effectively. This handbook the first executive self-coaching program that considers the operational area in order to fill all gaps from business leaders.

1. Overview of Handbook

This handbook is intended for the leaders, managers, and coaches who aspire to leadership excellence.

We believe this handbook is an absolute necessity if you have a vision to transform yourself and achieve great things in the future.

It contains vital content on coaching that is essential for you to transform yourself into the ideal leader you desire to be.

To be more precise, we present this handbook as a self-learning guide that can methodically support you in providing step-by-step coaching to support you on your transformational journey.

The handbook provides you with best practices, methodologies, and a step-by-step approach that is essential to improving your overall **productivity and performance**.

This handbook is designed in a manner that will allow you to engage in this **as part of your day-to-day job** by allowing you to make the best use of your time.

We would highly recommend that you go through the handbook completely to support you in achieving the best outcomes.

We wish you all the very best on your transformation journey.

1.1. What Is Executive Coaching?

Executive coaching is a process in which managers and leaders are guided to reflect and gain awareness of who they are and their potential strengths and weaknesses and guided in a structured manner to improve on essential areas in bringing the best out of them as a leader, utilizing their existing capabilities and resources.

Our Coaching Program is designed to support you in becoming a leader who is trusted by your employees. Furthermore, we will help you improve your influencing skills.

A trusted leader is a true influencer who can positively influence their employees to achieve the best outcomes for the organization. As part of our Coaching Program, we intend to bring the best out of you as a leader by teaching you to utilize a key set of skills that are highly desired for a leader.

Our approach to coaching is based on the two key fundamentals of **productivity and performance**.

1. Overview of Handbook

Productivity from an organizational context can be measured by how effective the employees are in delivering the desired outcome during a given period. Improving productivity has been the secret recipe for many organizations in achieving success.

As a leader, you will be tasked with goals, and your output is always measured by your performance. If you need to reach required performance levels, you will only be able to do so if you and your staff are operating at maximum productivity levels. Therefore, as part of our Coaching Program, we will coach you on improving your productivity to bring out the best performance from both yourself and your employees.

1.2. Why Executive Coaching Is Important

People have different skills and capabilities. However, there are certain important skills that organizations and employees expect from leaders. While subject matter expertise is vital, it is not sufficient in and of itself to be a successful leader in today's world.

Leadership requires some core skills that are mandatory for managing people successfully. In other words, there are some key qualities employees and organizations expect from a leader or certain things they look for.

Furthermore, another essential aspect discussed above is how a leader can improve **productivity**, which in turn contributes to improving **performance**.

Executive Coaching is critical because it will give you the necessary tools to transform yourself into the leader you can be, as many others have done in the past. As part of this handbook program, you will discover the areas that are essential to improve to help you to become a more successful leader by utilizing your capabilities and resources.

This handbook will guide you through a step-by-step approach to improving yourself in these key areas.

1.3. Can Executive Coaching Make Great Leaders?

Coaching is unleashing a person's potential to maximize their performance. It is motivational, which will influence your decisions and thought processes.

It is a mindset where you are influenced to do things in a more meaningful and methodical approach that will eventually help you bring out the best in yourself.

Being a good leader is a challenging task.

It is challenging because you need to be remarkably effective in one of the most challenging jobs you can have: managing people.

As a leader, you are always being evaluated on managing people and helping them achieve desired organizational outcomes. In simple terms, a leader should be exceptionally good at "getting things done" rather than "doing things."

However, to "get things done," you need to be good at influencing and challenging. You should be able to influence people positively to accept and face challenges with a positive attitude.

While you manage others effectively, you need to maintain your focus on your core job and responsibilities too. This is why you need advanced skills such as delegation and effective communication. As part of our program, we will coach you on these skills, along with many others.

Following is a simple illustration of what it takes to become a successful leader. This explains how positive influence, accommodation of challenges, and improving productivity can help in achieving desired performance.

1. Overview of Handbook

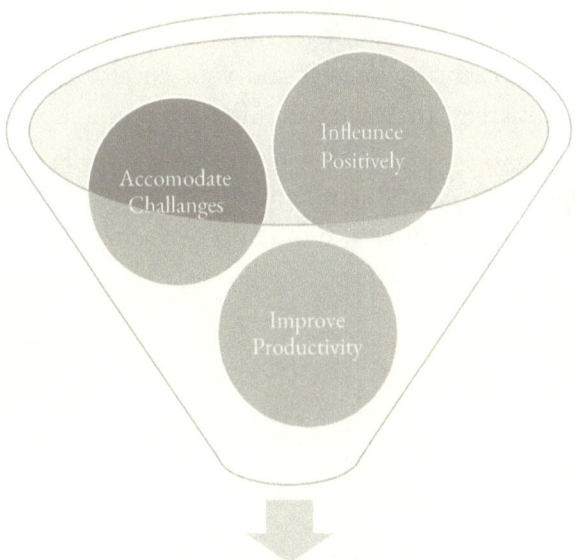

Achive desired performance

As part of this handbook, we will coach you through the processes and practices that will help you understand what it takes to become a great leader. We will provide you with in-depth knowledge and practices to bring out the best in you to become a successful leader.

However, coaching alone will not make you a great leader unless you are willing to implement what you learn. Therefore, we request that you practice the things you learn here in order to achieve the desired outcomes from this program.

Furthermore, you need to engage with your direct employees as part of your improvement process. Their feedback will be one of the most critical factors that directly impact your overall journey of transformation. It will be a key success factor not only at the beginning but will also be a key performance indicator toward the end of your journey.

Any feedback provided needs to be explored with an open mind to see if there is truly room for improvement. There is a strong chance that you may hear unpleasant feedback, and this could affect you negatively. Therefore, we encourage you to take such feedback positively even when it seems negative and try to determine how it can help you improve.

Following a period of time during which you feel you have made some modifications, re-evaluate yourself and your employees to see whether your change initiatives are having an influence on the updated feedback you are getting.

Find some employees you trust and try to continue this process until you and they see a clear difference and improvement.

2. Fundamental Areas of Focus

Following are the fundamental areas of focus in your self-coaching.

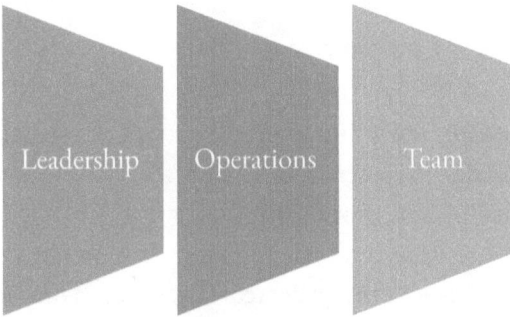

As we advance, we will guide you on the above areas in helping you understand how **productivity** could be improved on each of these areas that could eventually improve **performance**.

Furthermore, you will be guided on how to navigate challenges in **performance** and **productivity**, which is beneficial in your capability to "get things done" by your teams to give you the chance to focus on your executive job rather than just spending your time monitoring your team tasks.

Chapter One

3. Leadership

3.1. Who Is a Leader?

The word leader can have endless definitions. However, in our context, a **leader is a person who can lead people and processes in order to achieve business outcomes.**

Leaders need to be individuals who are self-motivated while they motivate others to achieve their expected outcomes. They are people who need to be filled with positivity, and they should be able to create a positive impact among the people around them. People need to be inspired by what they do and respect them for the positive impact they create. They should have a clear vision of what they have to achieve and strive toward it with passion and commitment.

Performance and productivity are two key components that a leader needs to keep improving throughout his journey as a leader.

3. Leadership

While being productive and achieving expected outcomes, leaders are expected to guide others to achieve productivity-driven performance.

In this handbook, we will highlight the most essential areas that a leader needs to focus on improving to go from a good leader to a great leader.

As per the quote, "**Leaders are not made, they are not born,**" our Executive Coaching Program is intended to challenge you to improve on key aspects that will allow you to transition from a **good Leader** to a **great Leader.** Furthermore, it is more appropriate to call this a **transformation** journey than to call it **transition.** This is because it not only transforms your work performance, but it also transforms you into a better individual.

With a careful and detailed analysis, we have identified a set of key skills that are essential to becoming a great leader. As part of the following sections, we will discuss in detail what each of these pillars is and why they are essential in your transformation journey.

Let us explore further, taking a deep dive into each of these areas.

3.2. Key Areas of Focus for Leadership

The following are identified as the key areas of focus for leaders.

Under each area, there are a set of key skills that leaders need to focus on.

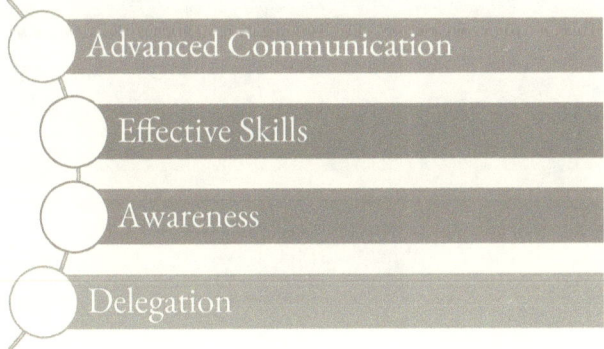

Each of the above areas will be further broken down into more logical and meaningful areas.

While each of these areas will be very familiar to many of you, we essentially focus on methods that can help improve the effectiveness of each that will eventually result in a productive outcome.

For a guaranteed outcome, we encourage you to refer to the following sections where we deep dive into each of these areas. You should make sure to put this guidance into practice to achieve the best outcomes.

3.2.1. Advanced Communication

To become a great leader, the very first area you need to focus on is communication.

While communication is an overly broad area to discuss, there are some key components that we will provide an additional focus on.

As you know, anyone who is identified as a great leader is also a good communicator. They may have different styles of communication, but they are always capable of attracting others and gaining the attention of their audience. If you have ever wondered how they do it so effectively, now is the time to get the answer to that question.

The following are areas of focus under **Advanced Communications.**

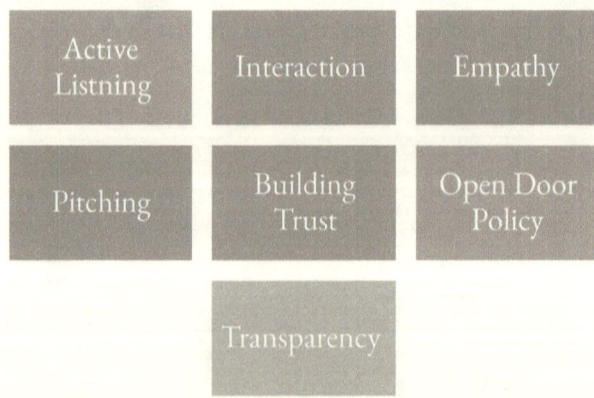

3. Leadership

In the following sections, we will be deep-diving into each of these areas.

Illustrated below is the methodology of the deep dive.

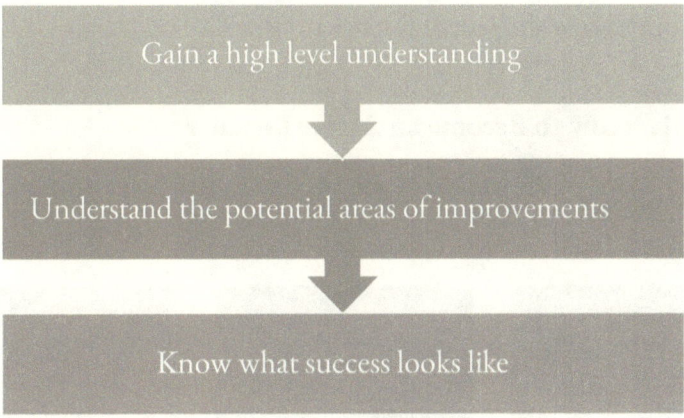

3.2.1.1. Active Listening

Communication is the heart of what we do every day in our lives, whether at work or at home. However, the habit of listening seems to be diminishing with the evolution of technology. Many of us are more comfortable spending time with our devices rather than communicating with people.

Active listening is an important aspect of advanced communication. Even though you may talk to people all day, active listening is a lot more than just hearing what they say.

From an organizational standpoint, active listening could be considered an attitude that allows a leader to listen to his fellow employees for the purpose of creating a shared understanding with a deeper attachment and respect for their emotions or feelings. While listening to the content of the conversation, it is even more important to understand the context, and it is also important to pay close attention to the employee's expressions and the emotions they reflect. Not only does active listening allow for seamless communication, but it also helps to solve problems or resolve conflicts in an amazingly effective manner. It helps a leader to pay closer attention to his employees and, in turn, gain their respect. It is natural for employees to respect a leader who listens to their concerns carefully and encourages them to communicate freely.

In the following sections, we will guide you in becoming an active listener or improve on your active listening skills.

3.2.1.1.1. How to Become an Active Listener

Below are some of the steps that you need to follow in becoming an active listener.

Before starting any conversation, make a conscious decision to give i t your full focus	Discipline your mind so that you do not get distracted by other thoughts	If you are busy, politely ask the employee to speak to you later when you
Put your cell phone away during conversations	Avoid checking the time (wristwatch or clock) while having a conversation	Avoid interrupting
Create a positive environment for employees to speak their mind	Avoid sarcastic comments during the conversation	Maintain eye contact and acknowledge what is said (i.e., by nodding or facial
Be patient when employees are underdoing emotional outburst	Respect the employee's emotions (i.e., congratulate them in a happy	Obtain clarification on areas that are not clear in a communication

3. Leadership

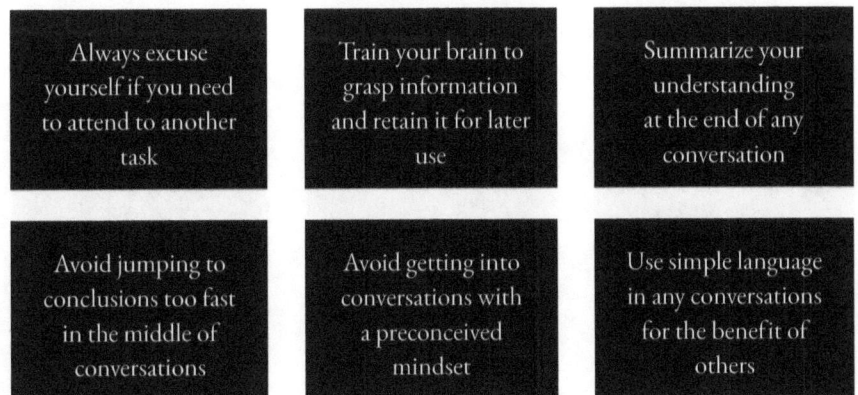

3.2.1.2. Interaction

Interaction means how well you collaborate and communicate with your employees. The most important aspect for a leader is his or her ability to get along well with employees. Workplace interaction is one of the most important skills a leader needs to focus on.

With the increasing trend of working from home, leaders need to make an effort to create room for interactions with employees virtually. This can be achieved by means of having a weekly catch-up call with different teams where the conversations are more casual and personal to understand what each employee feels about work and work pressure under the new normal.

Positive interactions with your employees will lead to many important insights for you. Furthermore, employees will feel an openness toward you and will eventually open up about their real challenges and issues. Such closer interactions could help gain valuable insights and eventually contribute to the growth of the organization.

This is something leaders need to practice on a continuous basis, and it **should never be a one-time exercise**. Continuous and consistent interactions are guaranteed to bring the best outcomes.

3.2.1.2.1. How to Improve Interactions

Make it a point to go to employees to discuss issues or address problems	Increase informal conversations with employees rather than formal meetings	Greet employees by name and always use positive body language
Be present in their workplace events	Keep communications simple, short, and meaningful for the benefit of everyone	Know whom you speak to level up conversations based on employee levels
Always go to the employees' location to share successes	Avoid correcting an employee in public. Keep these private.	Avoid using bad language even if you are frustrated or angry
Increase casual gatherings and outings to celebrate work successes	Make yourself easily approachable	Allocate a portion of your time to interactions with employees
Encourage a positive attitude between employees	Avoid displaying negative facial expressions during any interactions	Plan for various events that could improve workplace interactions
Encourage employees of different tiers to interact	Guide employees politely and privately on their interactions	Always thank employees for bringing up concerns and ideas

3.2.1.3. Empathy

Leaders need to always be mindful of the fact that not everyone shares their perspective. Remember that people are different and often see things from a different point of view than the leader or their manager.

Empathy is the ability to share and understand the emotions of others.

Empathy is an especially important skills for a leader because leadership as a role is mostly about dealing with fellow employees. For this reason, empathy is one of the most desired skills for a leader to have.

Something that is particularly important to understand here is that every human being is, by nature, empathetic. However, the levels of empathy may vary from one person to the other.

However, empathy is a skill that can be improved with some exercises and activities.

Empathetic leaders need to be able to understand a situation from the point of view of the person who is experiencing it. This helps the leader to understand the psychological aspects that could have contributed to this situation. **Empathy is extremely useful to a leader since it aids in the development of trust, respect, and good perceptions among employees.**

Leaders with empathy have proven to be capable of handling very complex problems or challenges effectively while coming up with solutions that are a win for both the company and the employee. **Furthermore, employees show a greater willingness to work with managers or leaders who make an effort to "walk in their shoes" and make an effort to understand them.**

3.2.1.3.1. How to Improve Empathy

Have a good understanding of yourself and your personality	Avoid having a preconceived mindset about your employees' emotions	Avoid judging people based on a single incident
Try to put yourself in their place to understand what they're going	Avoid comparing employees to each other	Don't let your biases control your decision-making
Gain an understanding of employees' personal life challenges	Smile more while interacting with the employees to create a more positive space	Try your best to address employees by name

3. Leadership

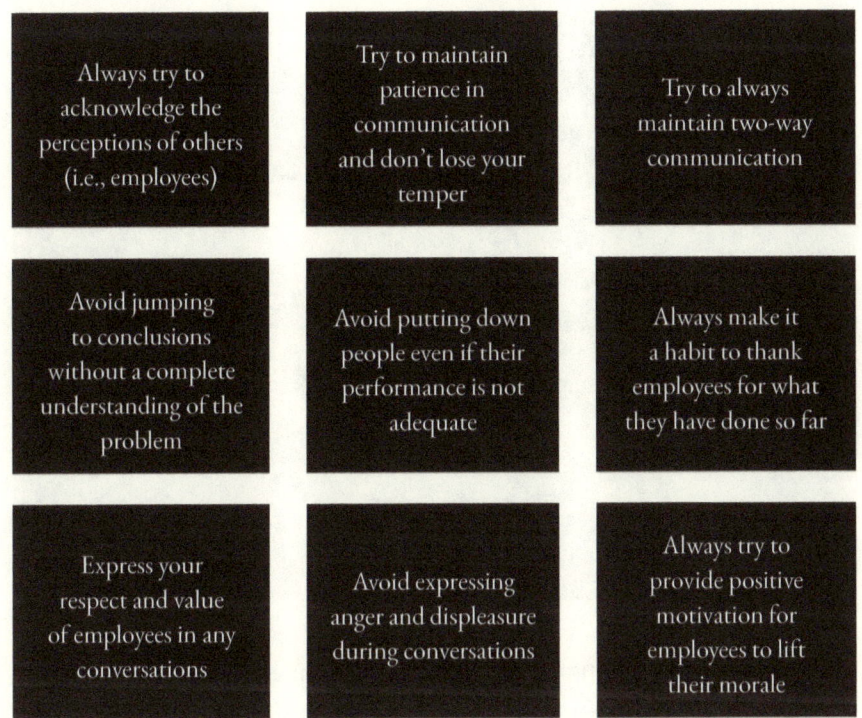

3.2.1.4. Pitching

Pitching is the ability to put forward a conversation or an idea in a way that will enable others to consider it positively. If you wish to become an inspiring leader whose ideas are appreciated by their customers and teams, pitching is what you need to work on. It is a skill that will help you gain popularity both within and outside the organization.

There is an exceedingly high chance that your employees and customers have endured hours and hours of boring conversations. Keeping their attention and focus is critical to achieving the results you desire.

Pitching is a skill that can be improved with adequate coaching. You need to keep your messages simple yet powerful. They need to have good energy to capture the attention of your audience. Furthermore, your communications need to be clear and correct. Carefully choose what to communicate so that your audience does not start questioning the validity and accuracy of your communication.

Practice is something that is key for a good pitch, but the time and effort you put in to master the art will pay off in the end.

3. Leadership

3.2.1.4.1. How to Improve Pitching

Know your audience before you initiate a conversation	Practice prior to any communication that you have with employees or customers	Keep your communications short, simple, and meaningful yet powerful
Drive conversations with a storytelling approach to relate it to the audience	Keep positive body language during communications	Avoid guessing or giving incorrect responses that will be easily disproven
Keep your conversations natural without rushing	Adapt to audience feedback and reactions to keep it more relevant	Avoid reading your content; take the time to learn it by heart
Carefully choose which questions you wish to answer and which to park for later	Avoid nerves taking control of you if you are faced with a difficult situation	Check your facts to avoid integrity concerns
Be mindful and remember each of your answers to avoid contradictions	Avoid underestimating your audience and their responses. Be prepared for the worst.	Show confidence in your communication with a solid tone and firmness in delivery

| Answer questions with relevant examples to increase clarity | Stay calm and casual and avoid displaying negative body language | End conversations with a powerful message or reminder to create a long-lasting impact |

3.2.1.5. Building Trust

Great leadership always begins with building trust at the workplace and among employees. Trusting relationships between leaders and their team members is the foundation of a successful organization. A leader who is trusted has more credibility and influence than one who is not. Furthermore, a trusted leader is can handle complex and challenging situations with ease. Employees tend to show more respect toward trusted leaders, and their words are given more consideration.

Character is the foundation for trust. It means holding high standards when it comes to values. Values make up a person. A great leader must be a person who is driven with great values.

Respecting your employees is one other important element that leads to creating a better impression among employees.

Leaders should not demonstrate themselves as someone who does not stick to their words or who tends to mislead their employees. This will only damage your reputation and could cost a lot in allowing you to correct problems. It is advised to avoid making commitments rather than

3. Leadership

making unrealistic ones, as this will lead to trust issues and potentially damaged goodwill.

While trust is a key element for better relationships within organizations, it is equally important for external business relationships as well. Customers and other businesses prefer trustable leaders over the ones with trust issues. Trusted leaders have better influence over their customers as well.

Building trust is a definite winning criterion for a leader who hopes for better outcomes.

3.2.1.5.1. How to Improve on Building Trust

Being honest in commitments and making sure they are met without fail	Being willing to accept responsibility for your own mistakes	Avoid taking credit for tasks that are done by someone else
Avoid practicing Divide and Rule methodologies among teams	Take genuine interest in your teams and their growth	Avoid overcommitting in any circumstance as it could lead to unfavorable outcomes
Avoid making accusations before getting all of the facts	Respond positively to follow-up questions about pending action items	Be there for your employees whenever they are need of your support or guidance
Empower the team and let them know they are trusted	Be transparent in conversations and when it comes to dispute resolutions	Always accept feedback and use it to make improvements

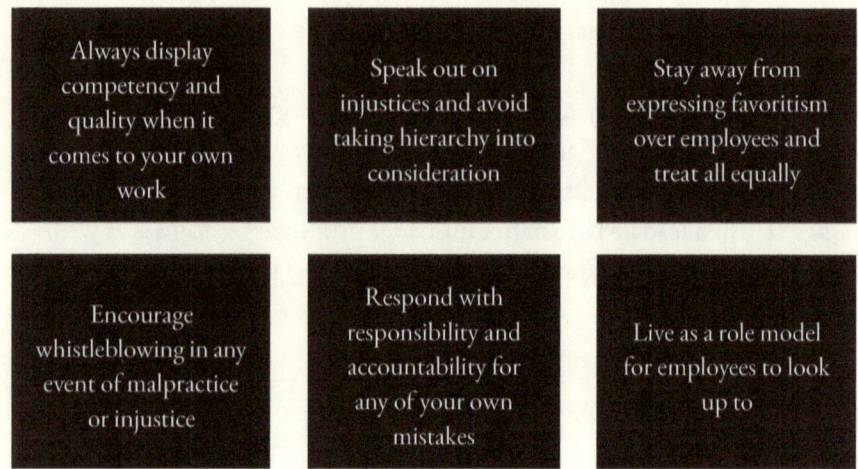

3.2.1.6. Open-Door Policy

Establishing an open-door policy in simple terms means that managers and leaders are always available to employees. They should also be in a positive mindset and a pleasant mood when having conversations with employees, especially if the employee has a problem or challenge. If the leader is not in a positive mindset, this could further worsen the situation of the employee, and the conversation is less likely to have a positive outcome.

The purpose of establishing such a policy in organizations is to encourage open communication. This would allow employees to walk into their manager's or leader's room to discuss any issues they face or any concerns they wish to raise. Establishing open-door policy policies will benefit organizations where important concerns and feedback are communicated to leaders and managers in a timely manner. This will assist managers and leaders to take necessary corrective actions and get things corrected or aligned. While some organizations have formally created such rules, there may be others where similar practices are used without explicit employee understanding.

It is highly recommended to communicate these policies clearly to employees to avoid creating any confusion because the employees who are

3. Leadership

unaware tend to assume the ones who are allowed this kind of conversation are being shown favoritism.

Such policies need to be ideally communicated to employees either as part of the on-boarding process or as a part of the Employee Handbook.

With the growing trends in remote working, this can be put to practice by leaders are managers being responsive to employee phone calls, messages, chats and be available to allocate time for a one-on-one virtual meeting.

3.2.1.6.1. How to Improve the Effectiveness of Your Organization's Open-Door Policy

Encourage more scheduled open door sessions than random ones	Set a preferred time and days to avoid work interruptions	Leverage effective communication tools to enable virtual conversations
Discourage room for workplace rumors and gossips	Improve awareness of the open-door policy	Address any ambiguities for improved clarity
Encourage teams for open casual communications apart from the formal communications	Obtain feedback from employees on what aspects should be improved	Encourage employees to walk in with the problem, along with some potential solutions too
Encourage multiple shorter conversations for problem-solving	Plan to set conversations with a maximum time slot	Create a positive environment for employees for an open conversation

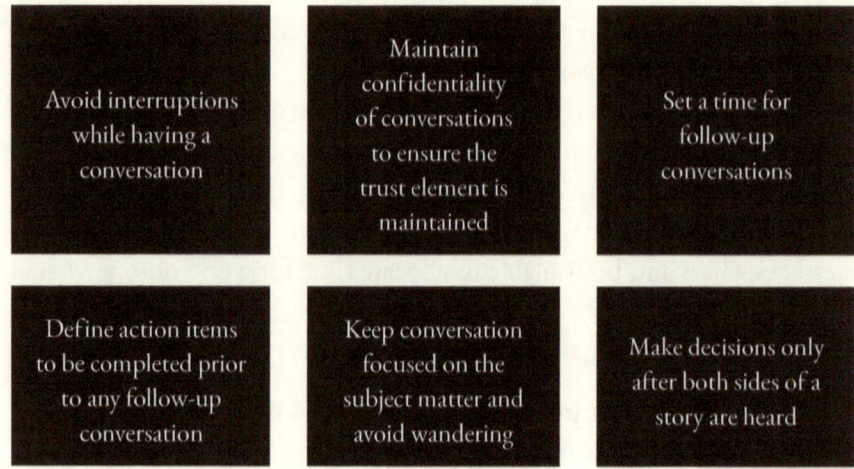

3.2.1.7. Transparency

Transparency at work means openness and honesty between the leader or manager and the employee. This is an especially important element because it encourages other aspects such as trust and positive communication, and it helps increase employee engagement.

Transparency should be a part of organizational culture. This is a culture that can be easily improved and enhanced for greater outcomes. Leaders and managers have a great role to play when it comes to improving transparency among employees in an organization. However, it is particularly important to understand that there is a very thin line between transparency and confidentiality. Both look alike; however, it is the duty of the leaders and managers to ensure that transparency is maintained in a manner where organizational confidentiality is maintained when it comes to important business strategies that have a major impact on the company if such news travels to the ears of unwanted individuals.

Due to this, leaders and managers should obtain clear guidance from the business stakeholders on which information is sharable and which is not. Once this is clear, for any information that is sharable, the relevant employees should be kept in the loop in any such communication. Furthermore, it is advisable to share any key decisions made with employees

3. Leadership

and explain to them why such decisions are made at an organizational level.

Leaders and managers should do their best to avoid surprises to the employees unless they are positive ones. Negative surprises could eventually lead to disillusioned employees, which could contribute to poor performance and outputs.

In addition to sharing information and being transparent, organizations should also encourage a culture where employees can question and obtain clarifications on important business decisions. Leaders and managers should be equipped with the required answers, and such communications need to be standardized and consistent to avoid each leader communicating the information in different ways that could lead to confusion among employees.

It is also important to allow and accommodate employee feedback in such instances because such feedback could support improving and fine-tuning business decisions.

Overall, transparency can bring substantial positive outcomes for organizations, and it is a key duty of the leaders and managers to ensure this culture is practiced in an effective manner to ensure it does not lead to any negative outcomes, as explained above.

3.2.1.7.1. How to Improve Transparency

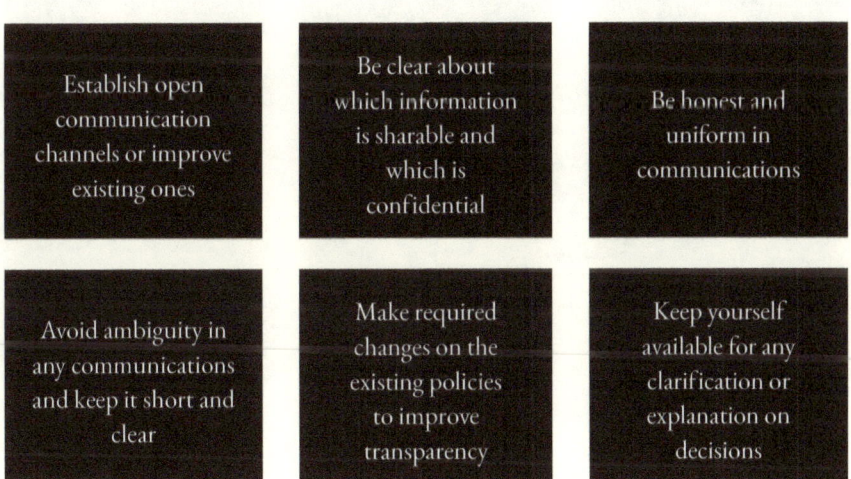

Coaching For Leadership

Make sure information is accessible to all employees at any given time	Have a positive attitude toward the input provided by employees	Always maintain your integrity in any communications
Always try to make collective decisions with respect to the views of others	Try to break down the silos in employee teams and groups	Define clear guidelines on communications among employees
Share both successes and failures with employees to keep them aware	Try to drive the transparency culture with the other employees	Choose tools and technologies to assist in maintaining transparency
Always try to have a point of view from an employee's standpoint before decisions are made	Improve visibility within organizational processes to employees	Avoid favoritism and bias

3. Leadership

3.2.2. Effective Skills

The second area that we will be focusing on Program is on effective skills that are essential for a leader in their journey of transformation from a good to a great leader.

One of the significant differentiators for a leader is their skills, which will allow them to bring desired outcomes of an organization.

While many leaders may already have these skills, we will essentially be focusing on how to effectively improve them to support you in your transformational journey.

Out of a lengthy list of effective skills, the following are some of the key ones we will explore further.

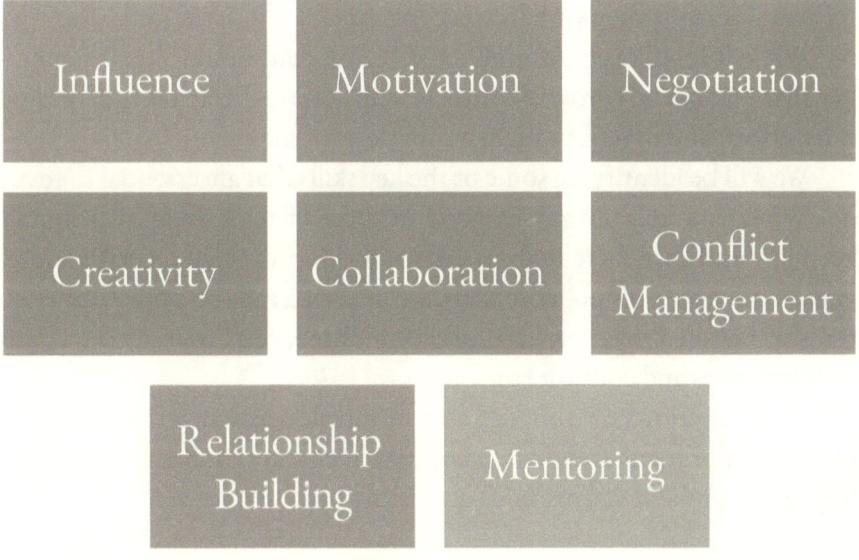

3.2.2.1. Influencing

Influencing in simple terms means the leader or manager's ability to move others into some action or activity. In other words, it means changing someone else's thought process and convincing them to carry out some task or a set of activities.

Influencing is one of the most important skills that any leader or manager can possess. You will be doing it daily.

To successfully influence others, a leader or manager first needs to prove themselves strong in their subject matter. Secondly, they must also have exceptionally good communication with the ability to stay positive.

It would be best if you can do well compared to others. Once you start to stand out from the rest, employees will start to look up to you.

While you improve on a range of soft skills from communication to command, you should focus on some other important aspects, such as dress code, body language, problem-solving methodologies, etc.

In an overall sense, you should be the best at many things. Once you get to this place, people will begin to look up to you as a thought leader, a mentor, someone they wish to work for, etc.

While it looks overly complex and broad, you should always remember that you cannot grow all of these skills overnight. It takes dedicated time, effort, and practice to achieve this level of mastery.

We will be identifying some of the key skills that are essential to focus on. While you may already be good in some of these areas, you should keep in mind that there is always room for improvement. Furthermore, you should not focus on more than two areas at a time on your journey of transformation. Once you have excelled in those, you can move on to two different areas and continue the process.

Avoid overloading yourself with multiple areas at a time, as it requires a lot of focus and dedication. When you are overloaded, you will have less focus and attention to detail, and you will not achieve the best outcomes.

3. Leadership

3.2.2.1.1. How to Improve Your Influencing Skills

- Improve your knowledge of your subject matter
- Always keep a positive attitude
- Lead by example and make yourself a role model
- Help people through the tough times
- Do not lose your energy and optimism
- Avoid showing anxiety to employees
- Always maintain your trustworthiness and honesty
- Avoid blaming the team for your shortcomings
- Accept responsibility for your mistakes
- Try to be authentic and develop your own unique style
- Be fair in your judgment and avoid favoritism
- Listen to any concerns brought up to you with an open mind
- Always present information backed with evidence for improved reception
- Avoid making decisions based on emotion
- Always have a logical and explainable reason for your decisions
- Avoid arguments and frame conversations on actions and outputs
- If you are challenged, accept it gracefully
- Maintain a pleasant attitude and body language

3.2.2.2. Motivation

Motivation is the ability of a leader or manager to take their employees to their achievement goals. We often see situations where people are de-motivated for various reasons.

As a leader, you may have employees complain that something is making them de-motivated. This is mainly due to their inability to keep themselves motivated, so you will need the ability to guide them through these challenging situations.

The first aspect any leader needs to excel in is keeping themselves motivated. Unless you are motivated, you will never be successful in motivating others. To keep yourself motivated, you need to focus on your goals. View mistakes as lessons and opportunities to improve how things are done.

If you ever come across a problem that you cannot immediately find a solution for, do not make up something off the cuff; rather, explain that you require some time to think it through carefully and then return when you have done so.

Ensure that your conversations don't de-motivate them further. If it's a problem you can provide a solution for, do it as quickly as possible. Even a verbal commitment might make the employee feel better.

Often, there is a remarkably close connection between de-motivation and appreciation. One of the key aspects of keeping people motivated is to make sure you recognize them for who they are and what they do. A simple acknowledgment can go a long way toward increasing employee morale.

Always keep an eye out for challenges your employees may be facing, and address them proactively instead of waiting for the employee to broach the topic. Have a positive attitude in any conversations and look for ways to help them overcome obstacles. Make them aware of the trust you have in them. These techniques will often result in the automatic removal of any de-motivation factors among employees.

In the next part, we'll go over some of the most important aspects of how to enhance your motivating abilities for greater results.

3. Leadership

3.2.2.2.1. How to Improve Your Motivation Skills

- Stay self-motivated and always have a positive attitude and body language
- Ensure timely recognitions of employees before it is too late
- Avoid overloading employees beyond their capacity
- Allow employees to express themselves with no interruptions
- Avoid blaming employees for their mistakes; rather explain how to do better next time
- Have regular conversations even when things are going smoothly
- Always envision the bigger picture and help them understand how important they are
- Avoid de-motivating employees when they do not achieve desired results
- Set achievable and reasonable goals
- Provide more responsibility with more authority
- Always stay focused on employee growth and take actions to achieve it
- Provide flexibility in decision-making with required guidance
- Encourage employees to come up with ideas and suggestions
- Combine recognition with financial perks whenever possible
- Always explain things from an end-objective /purpose standpoint
- Avoid microman-agement
- Create a positive work environment for employees
- Care about employees and show them respect and kindness

3.2.2.3. Negotiation

Negotiation can be defined as a conversation or dialogue between two parties to achieve a mutually favorable outcome. As a leader or manager, you will need to be extraordinarily strong in this.

Business is all about negotiation. It is a skill that is beneficial for handling both internal and external stakeholders.

In simple terms, whether it is an end-customer vendor, potential employee, or business stakeholder, negotiation is a key skill in all of these scenarios. While some individuals have inherent negotiation skills, many need to work to improve to achieve an effective level.

The objective of negotiation is to find a win-win solution for both parties.

Each negotiation will vary, and each should be treated as a unique situation. While experience in negotiation can help, you need to make sure you understand your decisions for each scenario, treating them as an individual scenario. Reusing a previous approach may not always bring you a desired result. To be a successful negotiator, you need to know who is on the other side of the table. It helps to prepare answers in advance to potential questions the other party may raise.

Furthermore, it helps to be aware of the other person's body language and tone to understand what their reactions are. Make sure you have a solid reason each time you put forward a suggestion for further negotiation. Avoid getting angry or frustrated as it may appear that you are inexperienced or immature.

In the following sections, we will be deep-diving into some of the key aspects of how negotiation can be improved.

3. Leadership

3.2.2.3.1. How to Improve Your Negotiation Skills

- Know your outcomes clearly before you step in to a conversation
- Carefully observe the other person or team in the things they do and say
- Have a neutral facial expression to avoid displaying your reactions
- Keep a neutral voice and a pace in communications
- Be strong and confident in putting forward your points
- Observe others' reactions carefully
- Do your homework to be prepared with background information
- Try to gain the attention of others and keep their focus during conversations
- Do not lay all of your cards on the table at once
- Put forward points that are logical and meaningful
- Strive for a fair negotiation and a win-win solution
- Respect others' views and respond logically and not emotionally
- Avoid losing your cool in a conversation or using inappropriate language
- Avoid getting offended when your views are logically defended
- Avoid getting into baseless arguments
- Know when it is time to walk away
- Avoid agreeing to terms that are favorable only in the short-term
- Avoid interruptions and wait until the other party finishes before commenting

3.2.2.4. Creativity

Creativity is something that is unique to each person. There are many ways where it can come through in a business setting. It is removing the normal boundaries of thought to come up with new problem-solving methodologies.

To make it clearer, a person may have a different point of view on how they see a problem and how they wish to find a solution. As a leader or manager, this skill will easily make you stand out from the rest.

Two key elements can contribute to your creativity. One of them is your deep knowledge of a specific problem or domain, and the other is your ability to think out of the box to come up with a unique solution that others might not consider. Creativity combined with subject matter expertise has often produced simple solutions to seemingly complex problems.

One of the key elements that needs to be in place for creativity is an unconstrained mind with the willingness to explore new things. If you are overwhelmed with your daily tasks, you will have less room for creativity.

Staying up to date with the latest technologies and innovations can easily contribute to your creativity because it will give you a whole new thinking paradigm. Sometimes it's much easier to enhance or finetune an idea than creating it from scratch. As a leader or manager, you must always have the drive to figure out new ways to do things smartly and effectively.

In the following sections, we will see in detail how creativity can be improved as a leader.

3. Leadership

3.2.2.4.1. How to Improve Your Creativity Skills

- Free your mind from routine work pressures
- Read and explore new innovations that are happening around the world
- See problems from a root cause perspective
- Encourage brainstorming both individually and within teams
- Fail fast and make failure inexpensive
- Try new ideas and methodologies often
- Search for ways to improve your current processes
- Try to replicate your successes in one area in other aspects of your business
- Be open to criticism and aware of de-motivators
- Co-create ideas and accommodate feedback from others
- Explore possible shortcuts to look for cost benefits
- Always stay positive and overcome the fear of failure
- Be positive and willing to take risks and challenges
- Drive creativeness among employees and reward for good ideas
- Read more on failures to avoid doing the same
- Engage your end consumers as part of your ideations to get their point of view
- Have continuous feedback during an entire process
- Celebrate success and encourage and reward employees

3.2.2.5. Relationship Building

Relationships are the fundamentals of business, both internally and externally. From an organization standpoint, your relationships as a manager or a leader directly impact your performance. Building strong and professional relationships with your employees means that they will go the extra mile to contribute to your success.

Human beings are naturally inclined toward positive relationships, whether socially or at work. People often tend to listen and respond well when they are being given directions from someone they have a good relationship with.

It has been noted that employees tend to leave managers and not organizations. The core factor contributing to an employee leaving their job is generally related to a manager with whom they do not want to work.

Building positive relationships is not something that is quite complex. However, it has a lot to do with the attitude of a leader or manager. People are quite different. Therefore, as a leader or manager, you need to keep in mind that you will face some challenges in building relationships. However, with a little practice, you will be able to overcome most of these quite easily.

On the other hand, you need to be very much focused on your external relationships too. These are mostly with business partners and customers. In the overall context, maintaining external relationships can be more complex than maintaining internal relationships.

EBPs (External Business Partners) (i.e., customers and vendors) by nature are quite demanding, and are not necessarily compelled to be nice to you. Furthermore, you have less control and influence over their point of view and attitudes. In the following sections, we will look at how you can improve your relationships with both employees and external stakeholders.

3. Leadership

3.2.2.5.1. How to Improve Your Relationship Building Skills

Be respectful to your employees and EBPs	See things from the other person's point of view	Avoid fault finding and rather try to work out a solution for the problem
Make efforts to express your appreciation of employees and EBPs	Show empathy in problem-solving	Dedicate time to work on relationship building strategies with both employees and EBPs
Make yourself approachable for both employees and EBPs	Try to be flexible in achieving positive and win-win outcomes	Be willing to accept a fair compromise if it helps achieve a quick resolution
Work on networking sessions with your employees and your EBPs on a regular basis	Include EBPs and employees in your seasonal gifts and bonuses	Allocate a budget for relationship building exercises on a regular basis
Connect your employees with your EBPs for better bonding opportunities	Try to always go an extra mile for your employees and EBPs in providing service excellence	Be accountable for your failures and always be willing to apologize
Always try to explain the root cause for a problem to your employees or EBPs	Learn lessons from past issues and avoid making the same mistake in the future	Always keep a positive and cheerful communication with employees and EBPs

3.2.2.6. Mentoring

Mentoring is an advisory relationship intended to guide an employee through certain development areas. As a leader or manager, one of the integral parts of your job role will be to mentor your subordinates. As a mentor, you are expected to have experience in a specific area that you wish to improve in your employee.

To become a successful mentor, you need to be clear on some of the potential areas you will be mentoring in. It would be best if you make sure you have the expertise to address any questions your employee may have.

While mentoring obviously benefits others, it can also enrich your professional career by helping you to fine-tune your existing skills. It will often help you develop new perspectives. Especially when you work with a less experienced person, you may gain a whole new understanding of how they see things and may give you a chance to correct your perceptions. Furthermore, it gives you satisfaction and motivation when you see success in others, especially those you were mentoring.

This is a skill that will improve over time. With more experiences and exposure, you will develop new insights and perceptions too.

One other important thing is to ask the employee or employees that you mentor for feedback. It is always possible that you will get new ideas that you can incorporate to improve your own processes and methodologies.

We strongly recommend that you to take any opportunity to mentor someone junior to you, and in the following sections, we will deep-dive into some areas of how we can improve on mentoring where you can transform from a good mentor to a great mentor.

3. Leadership

3.2.2.6.1. How to Improve Your Mentoring Skills

Understand your employee and adjust your conversation to his experience levels	Understand the strengths and weaknesses of your employee	Tailor your approach based on the individual personalities
Assist the employee during challenging situations	Be open to acknowledge different perspectives	Be open for feedback and incorporate relevant ideas for improvement
Learn, unlearn and re-learn new areas	Share personal experiences of overcoming obstacles	Improve your relationship with the employee to be more open and transparent
Offer constructive criticism to ensure you do not break employee confidence	Allow your employee to make decisions and provide guidance only if required	While you track employee progress, track your own progress too
Follow your own style without copying the mentoring styles of others	Embrace differences of opinions and avoid conflicting situations	Provide complete focus on mentoring and avoid multitasking
Continuously monitor progress and provide feedback for timely improvements	Practice humility and humor to keep things interesting for the employee	Maintain a relaxed pace and avoid displaying negative body language

3.2.3. Awareness

The third area of our focus is awareness. Awareness is an extremely broad area. As a leader, there are many of things you need to be aware of. Employees always look up to leaders when they have clarification or they would like to obtain an expert opinion. At such times, it can be quite embarrassing for a leader or manager to be unprepared to give clarifications. Due to this, we have identified some of the key areas that a leader needs to be aware of to ensure they do not encounter situations that would make them appear unprepared.

Following are some of the key areas of awareness that we cover as part of our program.

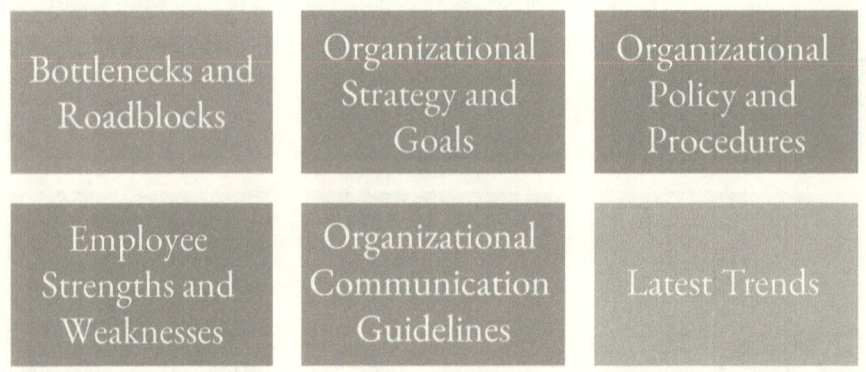

In the following sections, we will be deep-diving in to each of these areas.

3.2.3.1. Bottlenecks and Roadblocks

3. Leadership

Any organization, irrespective of its size or scale, has its potential bottlenecks and roadblocks. These are quite common, and there is not a one-size-fits-all solution. While some are addressed, they may appear again down the line in some other way.

Bottlenecks could be anything that potentially slows down an organization's process, eventually leading it to slow down or experience a drop in efficiency levels. This could either be due to a human being, a machine, a group of people, or a combination of machines and other equipment. If not, it could be due to the underutilization of resources or business process.

Bottlenecks can be addressed either by cutting down inefficiencies or by providing a workaround. There are two types of bottlenecks: internal (within the organization) or external (outside the organization). Internal roadblocks can be addressed much quicker than external ones due to the organization's ability to influence the situation. On the other hand, external situations may have higher complexity and challenges in comparison to internal ones.

Roadblocks can be both internal and external. However, the difference is that bottlenecks can be improved by improving efficiencies, but roadblocks are situations where some process had come to a standstill.

Leaders and managers need to focus on ensuring that their organization does not hit any roadblocks; prior arrangements and precautions should be taken to avoid them.

The potential damage from a roadblock could be multiple times that of a bottleneck. One common type of roadblock could be a sudden change in country regulations or the sudden imposition of a trade embargo. Therefore, leaders and managers have to ensure that proper risk mitigation plans are in place to ensure that these situations do not have devastating impacts on the business.

In the following sections, we will go into further details on how you can improve your awareness of these risks and take necessary corrective actions.

3.2.3.1.1. How to Improve Your Awareness of Bottlenecks and Roadblocks

- Keep a close eye on potential business embargos and trade restrictions
- Always have a plan B in the event that plan A fails for some reason
- Speak to employees to understand any challenges they currently face
- Review the existing business processes and take corrective actions to address inefficiencies
- Identify the key resources and make a succession plan for them
- Review and correct the business continuity plan on a periodic basis
- Identify skill gaps and train resources to improve efficiencies
- Brainstorm with department heads on potential ways to improve efficiency
- Remove bottlenecks by either amending the process or replacing the resources
- For external roadblocks, navigate through potential outsourcing options
- For legislation issues, seek for expert advice on effective navigations
- Build better relationships with government and legal entities
- Do ad-hoc audits to ensure things are going smoothly
- Review set KPIs, carry out required improvements, and track continuously
- Seek support on business intelligence tools for easy tracking of progress
- Execute plan B at times to ensure the business continuity is ensured
- Cross-train resources and do dry runs to ensure process continuity
- Reduce person dependability on key roles by periodic swaps of people

3.2.3.2. Organizational Strategy and Goals

Organizational strategy and goals are something all leaders and managers must be aware of in detail.

Occasionally, general employees may have access to this information. However, if you are a leader, you need to be in the loop. Organizational strategy may change on a short-term or long-term basis, and many business rethink their goals every year or five years. Due to the fast-changing market conditions, organizations may go through very rapid changes. All leaders need to be able to stay relevant and aligned with the organizational strategies. In such scenarios, it will be their duty to ensure that the changes are done as quickly as possible, and the relevant KPIs are set for the employees. To carry out such activities in a shorter period and to face questions and clarifications from employees, it is essential that you know what you are preaching.

Therefore, as a leader or manager, your ultimate duty is to keep yourself aware and updated of any organizational strategy changes and then to carry out an impact analysis to understand which goals and KPIs could potentially also change. Furthermore, it will be your duty to pass along these changes to your employees and create action items to ensure that the overall organizational objectives will be achieved.

Such rapid processes can have challenges of their own. Therefore, we recommend that all leaders make it a daily or weekly habit to check for changes and take the time to become thoroughly acquainted with them. Checking in with your peers is another way to make sure you are staying updated.

In the following sections, we will be doing a deep dive to understand how you can improve your awareness of such areas.

3.2.3.2.1. How to Improve Your Awareness of Organizational Strategy and Goals

Allocate time from your calendar on a periodic basis to read through changes	Discuss with your peers and subordinates to clarify any issues	Foresee potential change requirements of strategy and make adjustments in advance
Stay in touch with strategy teams on a continuous basis	Brainstorm with strategy teams on potential challenges and solutions	Educate your teams on changes to improve your visibility as well
Take questions from the employees to strategy teams to obtain clarification	Keep in mind the core pillars of strategy points and vision and mission statements	Always align your conversations to organizational strategies to stay relevant
Volunteer to attend brainstorming discussions or workshops	Revisit goals and make suggestions for improvements and finetuning	Discuss and create awareness of goal changes for better visibility
Be open for feedback on goals from employees and incorporate any fair amendments	Review employee awareness and their own goals on a periodic basis	Stay updated with the communication guidelines of the organization
Carry out a self-assessment to check your awareness of strategy and goals	Gamify the learnings on strategy and goals to make it more engaging	Take measures for those who fail to update themselves on personal goals

3. Leadership

3.2.3.3. Organizational Policy and Procedures

Organizational policies and procedures are the guidelines that every employee needs to be aware of. A policy is a document that contains the operation procedures and guidelines that all employees need to follow based on their job roles and functions. As a leader or manager, you need to be aware of all policies. While these can be lengthy documents with long lists of items, you must allocate time to read, understand, and be able to interpret them clearly.

Based on the size and nature of the organization, the number of policies and procedures will vary. However, for any given organization, there will be some that are common for all teams. For example, rules for time off or communications could be general. These need to be given top priority.

Secondly, each department will have their own specific policies and procedures that are specific to them and vital to understand. As a leader, you have to stay updated and relevant with both of these policy types.

Thirdly, there could be other policies that are occasionally important, such as for foreign travel, which is important if you are planning a trip. These should be read and understood as the situations arise.

While you are aware of the policies, there are many times when there will be updates and amendments. In such cases, you need to make sure you do not fail to update yourself on such changes and the areas that are being impacted. Once you are up to date, your next responsibility is to ensure that your departments and subordinates are aware of them. It is mandatory that you make it a point to check your team's awareness. In the event of any issues, it will be your duty to ensure you take necessary corrective actions to address these gaps in understanding.

In the following section, we will be doing a deep dive to understand how to improve your awareness of the organizational policies and procedures.

3.2.3.3.1. How to Improve Your Awareness of Organizational Policy and Procedures

Allocate time to learn organizational policies and procedures	Keep track of changes and be aware of specific updates	Prioritize the policies and procedures per your job functions
Evaluate how the changes could impact business processes	Brainstorm policy changes with your team for potential challenges	Highlight any challenges to the relevant business stakeholders
Always be positive with employee feedback on policy changes and terms	Revisit policies to validate its relevance and identify potential amendments	Check for department level standard operating procedures (SOPs) for updates
Allocate time for employees to go through relevant policies and procedures	Gamify the learning process to make it interesting	Test employee awareness on the policies and guidelines
Improve awareness among employees on why they need to adhere to these	Remove ambiguity from the Policies and Procedures	Carry out interactive discussions with teams in Policy and Procedure Reviews
Carry out a self-awareness check on policies and procedures	Initiate assessments to validate awareness on a periodic basis	Link this to a KPIs to ensure employees are taking it seriously

3. Leadership

3.2.3.4. Employee Strengths and Weaknesses

Leaders and managers are the custodians for their employees. Therefore, it is their duty to ensure they are up to date on who their employees are and their key strengths and weaknesses. Remember that each employee is unique, and their skills and capabilities will be different. For example, while one employee is good at communications, they may not be so great when it comes to execution.

An organization requires people of different talents and skillsets. However, expecting all skills from one individual is not practical. A successful leader or a manager can accurately understand the skills of each individual and position them in a role or task that can make the best use of their strengths. At the same time, It is also very important not to call attention to their weaknesses, as it could negatively impact their morale and job performance.

As a leader or manager, you must be clear about which skills are required for each job and how your employees can meet these needs. This is the first level of filtration that you must be exceptionally good at.

As the second step, you should be good at understanding the potential skill gaps faced by each employee and how this can be improved for them to effectively do their jobs.

At the third step, you must be clear on the weaknesses of employees, and you need to discuss with them how those can be improved gradually. While some skills can be improved, some aspects are resistant to change. Therefore, it is your responsibility to figure out what can be worked on and then devise a plan with the employee to implement these changes. This can be quite challenging, but if the employee is willing to try, you have to create the right environment for them to go through this journey.

In the following section, we will deep-dive into some areas to understand how you can improve your awareness of your employees.

3.2.3.4.1. How to Improve Your Awareness of Employee Strengths and Weaknesses

- Engage closely with your employees
- Obtain feedback from direct managers on employees' strengths and weaknesses
- Carry out periodic assessments of employee strengths and weaknesses
- Cross-train the employees to figure out if there can be any improvements
- Provide a performance improvement plan to improve on key skills
- Identify potential weaknesses of employees and work on corrective actions
- Provide upskilling opportunities for employees
- Allow employees to transfer within business units if they are proven capable
- Pay special attention to key employees who are strategically important
- Have one-on-one conversations with employees about their weaknesses
- Understand the root cause of the weaknesses and address it
- Work to improve the confidence levels of employees
- Recognize their efforts to improve on weaknesses
- Identify the potential gaps of knowledge for upskilling requirements
- Mentor the employees in a friendly manner to overcome any challenges
- Create teams with multiple skills to meet organizational needs
- Set KPIs and measure them closely for better outcomes
- Frequently revisit benchmarks to keep improving continuously

3.2.3.5. Organizational Communication Guidelines

Communication guidelines mean a set of procedures and guidelines that any official communication needs to adhere to. They are an especially important requirement for any organization. While some organizations have incredibly detailed guidelines, some organizations may not have many in place. However, as a leader or manager, you need to understand and adhere to your organization's communications protocols.

Once again, this may vary from one organization to another. While many organizations have communication guidelines for external and internal communications, some may only have one of them. Irrespective of the communication guidelines, it is always advisable that you consult leadership before any official communication is made. If there are clear guidelines in place, your first duty is to make sure that you are fully aware of the organization's communication protocols. If you do not adhere to these, it could lead to problems, especially when you represent your organization. It is always good to be prepared for frequently asked questions.

Furthermore, it is also very important when you communicate within your team. It is always recommended to let the communications teams check official communications within organizations. When this is not possible, it is recommended that you acquire the right communication materials from the respective teams and ensure that they are communicated.

3.2.3.5.1. How to Improve Your Awareness of Organizational Communication Guidelines

- Stay updated with any recent changes to communication guidelines
- Discuss communication guidelines with teams for knowledge sharing
- Validate communication compliance for any communications made
- Highlight any unclear ambiguous areas in guidelines for clarification
- Suggest changes or areas of improvement
- Validate team's awareness of guidelines on a timely basis
- Review past non-compliance to avoid it in the future
- Implement damage control for any potential non-compliance
- Review employee handbook coverage on communication guidelines
- Obtain feedback from employees on the communication guidelines
- Enable easy accessibility to communication guidelines
- Figure out root cause for common non-compliance of communications
- Carry out quizzes to validate if employees are updated on recent changes
- Create awareness on why communication guidelines should be followed
- Use anonymous suggestion forms for improvements
- Carry out periodic internal and external surveys
- Set targets to address gaps in communication guidelines
- Apply hypothetical scenarios to check if you are following guidelines

3.2.3.6. Latest Trends

We live in a world where things are changing quickly. Every day we see some innovation or trend that takes us all by storm. As a leader or manager, it is particularly important that you stay updated with the latest trends. Some of those may directly impact on your industry or job, while others could be general information or knowledge that may help you indirectly. While you spend time focusing on your core job, make it a habit to allocate some time to check out what is happening around you. With the help of technology, things have become easy and fast to implement.

You may want to follow social media pages that talk about technology and innovation or subscribe to newsletters or journals relevant to your specific field. Furthermore, if your organization has internal communications that are relevant, ensure that you allocate time to keep up with those. Understanding the latest technological trends that support the efficiencies and productivity of businesses are some key areas that leaders and managers need to focus on.

Businesses that stay on top of transformational trends will always have an advantage over those that don't. First mover advantage is a reality that no one can deny. You need to be a change agent who implements trends that will help improve your employees' efficiency and productivity levels. Make it an organizational culture and encourage your employees to stay updated. Explain that it will benefit them to develop their skills and advance their career with the organization.

Innovation has to be a main area for any organization. It never stops, and there is room for improvement even in the your most efficient business processes.

Out-of-the-box thinking combined with innovative mindsets has been proven to produce greater outcomes.

3.2.3.6.1. How to Improve Your Awareness of the Latest Trends

- Follow the news for the latest innovations around the world
- Watch what your competitors do better and adopt what is relevant
- Review key failures of your competition to avoid it in your workplace
- Identify what disrupts your industry as a whole
- Engage with people who are positive toward innovation and change
- Learn new technologies and methodologies
- Ask for support if you think you need help in understanding a new trend
- Drive innovation among all employees and at all levels
- Try things in a new way to see if it is an improvement
- Obtain expert opinion when it comes to rolling out new methodologies
- Create awareness among employees of such new trends or methodologies
- Learn what leading companies in the world are doing
- Visit successful companies to see what they do
- Sign up for innovation workshops
- Volunteer yourself for thought leadership teams
- Make reading a habit and allocate time for it
- Learn about technological threats and security breaches
- Join volunteer associations around the latest trends

3. Leadership

3.2.4. Delegation

The fourth area of our focus is delegation. Unless you master the art of delegation, it is highly unlikely to grow as a successful leader.

Delegation can be identified as the process of getting things done by someone else. While it seems extremely easy on the surface, effective delegation is a complex task that only a few succeed at. It is an art to delegate a task to the right person at the right time to ensure the desired results are achieved.

Listed below are our core areas of focus as part of understanding what effective delegation is. We will be doing a deep dive into each in the following chapters.

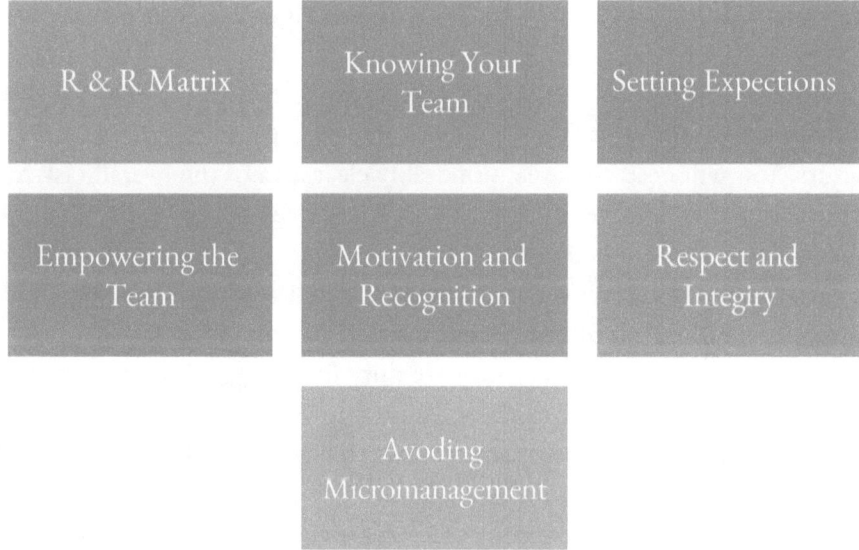

3.2.4.1. R & R Matrix

The roles and responsibility matrix is one of the most important tools a manager has when delegating. A comprehensive R&R matrix contains details on each role and its responsibilities. This is also known as the RACI matrix.

Responsible: The person doing a given task.

Accountable: The person who is accountable for a given task. Most of the time, the accountability lies with the supervisor.

Consulted: This can be anyone who is consulted when this task is being done.

Informed: This includes anyone who needs to be informed of the task's progress. It could be different stakeholders and different levels.

The R&R matrix can be extremely helpful as it clearly defines a task from various dimensions. As a leader or manager, you need to understand that a single task may require many people's inputs and acceptance to be successful. In the absence of an R&R matrix, it will be quite challenging to track who needs to do what and how the responsibility is spread out. While one person is doing the task, more responsibility lies with the person who approves it. This is the reason why organizations have supervisors. You will need to have a noticeably clear idea of the overall task to ensure that it will deliver its desired outcomes. Lack of clarity on this area could always lead to chaos.

In the following sections, we will see in detail why the R&R matrix is important and how it can help you in your delegation process.

As a leader or manager, your core duty in the organization is to ensure you get work done by others. In getting work done by others, one especially important aspect that you need to have is a 360-degree view of is who is doing the task and who is approving the work. Additionally, you need to know who is being consulted or providing input and who your potential stakeholders are.

Now let's try to understand how each component on the R&R matrix can help you in an effective delegation process.

Responsible: You must have a clear idea of who is responsible for a task. When it comes to assigning a task, you always need to you know to whom you are assigning it and if that person is capable of doing it. Unless you have this clarity, you could assign a task to anyone just from their job role and designation.

The benefit of an effective delegation is that in addition to the designation or the job role, you will get a closer look at his strengths and weaknesses. While two people can hold the same designation, one could be a person who is effective in communication while the other person might not be. In such a scenario, if you were to assign a task that involves much communication to a person who is not so great at it, the final result or outcome might not be so great that you could achieve by assigning it to the person who is good at it. Therefore, it is always important to ensure that you find the right person for the task if you have a selection to choose from.

Accountable: Understanding who is accountable for a task is mandatory to ensure a quality outcome. Accountability means taking ownership of the task's final delivery. While the task is done by someone junior, the accountability usually lies within the department head or an immediate supervisor of the responsible person. The accountable person must ensure they do a thorough check to ensure that the task delivered meets expectations from all angles or getting it re-done by the responsible person.

The accountable person acts as a quality gate to ensure it meets the set exit criteria to be recognized as a successful output. As a leader or manager, you must always ensure that you make the right people accountable. Failing this could lead to serious output issues with deviations in expectations vs outcome.

Consulted: Different tasks may have different levels of consultations involved which may vary from one organization another. However, it is important to understand who is being consulted for a task's completion.

There are exceedingly high chances for a task to go wrong if the wrong people are consulted. Here is an example.

Let's assume the task is office relocation, and the admin manager is tasked to come up with a relocation plan where he is made responsible for the plan and the senior admin manager is made accountable for the plan.

However, while both the admin manager and his senior can work on an incredibly attractive relocation plan, it is particularly important to consult with the right people. In this case, it could be the department heads who are part of this relocation. For some reason, if they are missed or the incorrect person is spoken to, there is a chance they will be given some inaccurate information that may result in an error on the plan.

Therefore, as a leader or manager, you have to ensure that each person is interacting with the right people so that the right input is provided for a successful outcome.

Informed: When it comes to any organization, it is less likely that top business executives (i.e., CEOs or owners) will get involved in individual business tasks. They will be mostly delegating the tasks to others, and they will only be interested in the outcomes and any potential challenges or issues.

As a leader or manager, you must make sure you do timely updates to the business stakeholders of a task's progress. The frequency of updates and the level of detail vary based on the task. Furthermore, the stakeholders for a task could also vary from one task to another.

As a responsible leader, it will be your duty to make sure that you keep the right people in the loop when it comes to any such communications and updates. Therefore, you need to understand the task and its stakeholders to ensure you are sending updates to the right people at the right time. Furthermore, you need to ensure that communication channels are properly defined, and the team is tasked with action items periodically for the updates.

3. Leadership

3.2.4.1.1. How to Improve on the R&R Matrix

Improve getting to know the employee	Focus on the key strengths of employees	Understand the reasons for the key weaknesses of the employees
Speak to employees one on one about how to improve on weaknesses	Introduce a plan for improving key weaknesses	Focus on finetuning the key strengths of the employees periodically
Conduct periodic reviews on employees' improvement plans	Segment employees into groups based on their strengths and weaknesses	Be conscious of strengths and weaknesses in task allocations
Revisit the job descriptions of the roles to assess the practicality of goals	Review and update the R & R of the jobs to stay on par with market demands	Encourage employees to shadow a different role to explore strengths
Share management best practices with the employees	Take the time to find the unique skills of each employee	Minimize overburdening employees who are reliable
Obtain feedback from employees on how they feel about their R&Rs	Provide realistic solutions for the problems highlighted on R&Rs	Encourage employees who strive hard to achieve their assigned R&Rs

3.2.4.2. Knowing Your Team

As a leader or manager, your team mostly defines your success. One of the greatest assets for a leader is their team.

Everyone in a team is different. Unity in diversity is one of the key points of success. Knowing your team means knowing each individual in your team. You need to know their strengths and their weaknesses. Furthermore, you need to know their personalities and their emotional challenges too. While this can be a time-consuming task, over time, you will be able to gain a very good understanding of each individual.

Continuous interaction with your team is a definite accelerator for this task where it helps you up to speed up the process. Each interaction with your team is an investment providing you with more insights into of who your team members are.

Each individual may have different skills, and their endurance levels may vary. While an individual could be very attentive to detail, his ability to cope with stress might be very poor, and on the other hand, there could be another individual who has very good endurance where failures may not have any negative impacts on his dedication levels.

Therefore, you need to ensure that you engage with the team through various situations and scenarios to gain a complete understanding. In the following section, we will see why it is important and how this understanding can be used effectively in task delegations.

Every day is a new day, and every business challenge is unique too. Therefore, you must match the right tasks with the right individuals to achieve good outcomes. While the task is the same, different situations and contexts may require special skills to achieve success.

Let's look at an example. Let's assume you are a company that specializes in selling computers. You have an opportunity from a customer, and you are expected to do a product demo. While you have many sales executives who could effectively demonstrate your products, one key challenge is that the client is someone who is identified as a difficult client, known for losing his cool.

In this kind of situation, while you have many sales executives, the right person will be someone who has handled tough customers and can

3. Leadership

maintain their patience and professionalism in front of a customer who easily loses his cool.

While a typical delegation would be to send any sales executive, an effective delegation would be to make sure you find the right executive who fits the need and give him or her some background on the customer, which will help them be prepared for a potentially tough conversation. If you do such an effective delegation, it is more likely to deliver positive results than a typical delegation that is done without much consideration for each individual scenario.

3.2.4.2.1. How to Improve on Knowing Your Team

Learn all employees' names if possible	Maintain continuous employee interaction irrespective of hierarchy	Conduct unplanned and informal chats with employees
Make employees feel valued by involving them in key discussions	Allocate breaks during the day to speak to employees as a regular practice	Try to conduct calls and meetings on video mode to keep it more interactive
Speak to employees about the challenges they face at work	Obtain continuous feedback from employees on the organization's successes and failures	Help employees become comfortable speaking to their leaders
Try to minimize the fear factor employees have about leaders	Be open to criticism and avoid taking it personally	Always try to respond with points and logic but not with authority and power

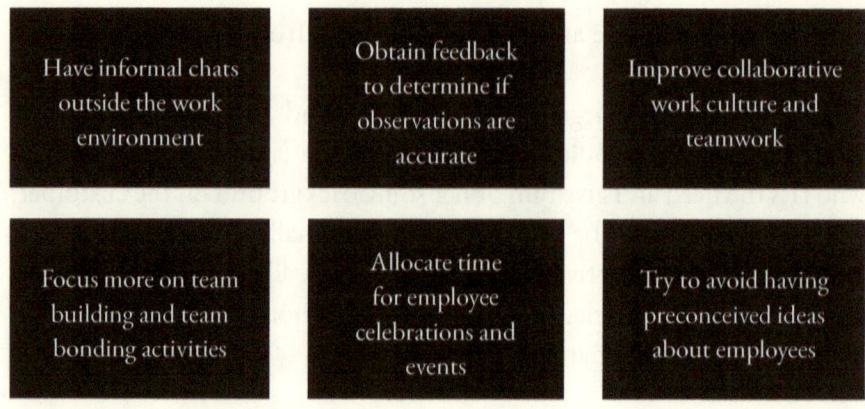

3.2.4.3. Setting Expectations

Setting expectations means determining the right objectives. As a leader or manager, one of your core duties is to set the right expectation for each employee. Unless the expectations are clear, there is a high chance that the employees will not perform as you would like them to.

While employees have their designations and job descriptions, they are more likely to change as per organizational requirements on a case-by-case basis. When it comes to setting expectations, you need first to understand the gaps in expectations. To figure these out, you need to be in close contact with department heads and immediate supervisors. Once such gaps are identified, you can decide how to address them. Furthermore, you need to have a clear understanding of how addressing such gaps could lead the employees to deliver what is expected of them.

After these are identified, you need to either have a conversation with the employee or their immediate supervisors to communicate the organization's expectations. While some employees may understand these communications clearly, there is a chance that the employees might either not accept the expectations or may assume that they are already meeting them.

When the employees have disagreements, you need to be very firm in your communication about why the organization has such expectations. Furthermore, you should be able to articulate in a polite manner the consequences of the objectives not being met.

3. Leadership

If the employee believes they are already meeting the organization's expectations, you need to help them understand the gap in their delivery versus the expectations. Once the employee understands, there must be continuous monitoring to ensure the expectations are met.

As each employee is unique, there can be a difference in how long it may take to deliver the set expectations. It is especially important to understand if the employee is making a clear effort. If a clear effort is being made, you need to support the employee by providing the necessary guidance on a timely basis to assist them on their journey.

In situations where the efforts are not made or are not visible, it is recommended to have conversations with the employee and figure out the root cause for the lack of visibility and address it on a case-by-case basis.

In the following section, we will see more details as to why setting expectations is important for effective delegation.

Simply delegating a task does not ensure that the right output will be delivered. If you are a leader who is effective in your delegations, it is critical that you always set the right expectations for your employees. Not setting the right expectations will result in outcomes with gaps, and the resolution of this will always involve time and a lot of effort, especially if it demands a rework.

Once the right expectations are set, things always become easier as you have mitigated the risk of the potential gaps in outcomes to a greater level. Furthermore, employees will also find it extremely easy to work, and there are fewer chances for disappointments due to the potential gaps in outcomes.

The key benefit of setting expectations for ineffective delegations is that it always has greater chances to deliver good outcomes and positive results. This is particularly important as any potential rework could cost both time and money. While cost can sometimes be recovered, time is an aspect that can never be recovered.

However, even with correct expectations, employees occasionally do things wrong. This could be due to carelessness or a simple misunderstanding. As a leader or manager, you need to keep a close eye on employees who are prone to this. You may even need to monitor them on a stage-by-stage basis to ensure that the process is moving in the right direction. This can be amazingly effective because it allows room for corrections before mistakes become serious. Furthermore, any gaps can be identified early in the process, making them less impactful.

One other important aspect to keep in mind is that with the right mindset and guidance, you can learn from your mistakes in order to avoid making the same mistake once again. Therefore, it is highly recommended that you apply the lessons you've learned and apply them to future projects. Everyone can learn from this and the work can improve to a level where you can be happy with the outcomes.

Finally, one especially important aspect many leaders and managers focus less attention on is the feedback process. Feedback is a crucial piece that can solve many issues in employee expectations and outcomes. You need to make it a routine practice to obtain employee feedback so you can prevent issues with clarity.

While employees can be unique, the same may be applicable for the managers or leaders too. There are times where as a leader, you may not be clear enough in what you communicate, or you might not be effective when it comes to setting expectations, or you could be ambiguous in your directions.

While you assume yourself to be perfect, you may not be as good as you think. Therefore, it is always recommended that you obtain continuous feedback from your employees to see if they are clear with what you say or if there are any areas of improvement that they feel are essential.

While feedback will vary from one employee to another, you should take it in a positive light. Nothing is more helpful than hearing what people think of you or pointing out your potential improvement areas. Once this information is collated, you can carefully choose which aspects are important and then devise a plan to address those areas.

Once you are making efforts to improve on an area, it is always good to check with your employees to see if they can see a difference. As an example, let's assume you are being told that you speak too fast and that employees find it difficult to understand what you say. In such a situation, the corrective actions would be to slow down and speak at a moderate speed. Once you feel you are doing it right, go back to your employees and ask if they now see an improvement in your ability to make yourself understood. Then if you still identify any gaps, you will need to take more corrective actions to address them effectively.

3. Leadership

3.2.4.3.1. How to Improve on Setting Expectations

- Improve practicality when expectations are set
- Discuss with employees when certain expectations are set
- Apply past lessons learned
- Communicate set expectations and ensure that they are clear
- Identify potential bottlenecks in achieving expectations
- Consider employees strengths and weaknesses when expectations are set
- Consider and account for potential risks when expectations are set
- Come up with mitigations for potential risks while setting expectations
- Try to always have an alternative plan if the expectations ae not met
- Closely monitor the set expectation and the progress in achieving it
- Take timely corrective actions in the event that there are deviations in achievement
- Consider a contingency for actions beyond your control (i.e., pandemic, etc.)
- Do a root cause analysis for unmet expectations as part of lessons learned
- Focus on key areas of improvements based on lessons learned
- When expectations are met successfully, further finetune to make it better next time
- Avoid ambiguity in setting expectations
- Use simple language to explain the expectations
- Reset expectations if the set expectations do not provide desired outcomes

3.2.4.4. Empowering the Team

Delegation and team empowerment are two aspects that work hand in hand. Team empowerment means giving the required authority to the team in making some of the key decisions.

Often, employees are faced with situations where they will be required to obtain approvals and instructions from their managers or leaders in decision-making processes. While this has its benefits, it could also have its drawbacks. As a leader or manager, you must empower your team to do their jobs. Empowered teams usually have high morale, and the employees will be self-motivated as well. Team empowerment trickles down to individual empowerment of employees.

When you work on team empowerment, you must always have a very good understanding of the potential challenges or roadblocks the team or the individuals face in executing their jobs. Once these are identified, you need to do a deep analysis to understand how much of that task can be done by the employee instead of going back and forth for approvals. This needs to be carefully defined to ensure that it does not lead to a situation where empowerment could significantly impact the business. Furthermore, it is recommended to take a phased approach where the empowerment is done as a step-by-step process.

Given below is one such example for a clearer understanding of how this can be effectively implemented.

Let's assume that employees who work long after the usual office hours must obtain approval from their managers. One way you can gradually empower the employees would be if an employee wants to work an extra hour, they do not need to obtain approval. If their time exceeds more than an hour, approval is needed. Over a period, you should be keeping track of the outcomes to see if the late hours bring in any productive outcomes with simple objectives. Once you identify this, you can now gradually push the bar a little higher by making the no-approval limit two hours.

It is advisable to do it gradually so that you are aware of the impacts of what you are doing and build the confidence of the employee, ensuring that there isn't any misuse of the empowerments provided.

3. Leadership

As explained above, both delegation and empowerment work hand in hand. There are two key components that are important to discuss regarding the delegation and its relativeness.

As a leader or manager, whenever you assign a task to an employee, you need to make sure that the employee is empowered to perform the assigned task. In situations where an employee is not empowered, this is more likely to create issues where employees become frustrated and feel overburdened.

On the other hand, you also need to ensure that the employees are not over-empowered. In the previous section, we discussed gradual empowerment. This is important because if employees are over-empowered, one wrong decision could put the entire organization at risk. Therefore, empowerment is something you need to tackle very carefully to ensure it is done at the right time to the right level.

Delegation of tasks tends to be quite easy once you empower an employee to the right level. This is because empowerment makes employees feel good about themselves. This increases their morale and self-confidence. They will start to feel that they are being recognized. These are critical factors that drive employee happiness and loyalty.

Happy and loyal employees almost always go the extra mile to get their desired results, and these employees always tend to deliver something exceptional that exceeds expectations. Such situations are potential growth factors for an organization and result in greater outcomes.

Therefore, our recommendation to you is always to do your quick check to see if the employees are empowered to the right level to carry out the tasks they are delegated and if not, make sure to do the right empowerment before a delegation to assure greater outcomes.

3.2.4.4.1. How to Improve on Empowering the Team

- Understand the team strengths and capabilities
- Assess the pros and cons of empowerment
- Empower timely and carefully, assessing overall context
- Choose carefully whom to be empowered and to what level
- Provide the required empowerments to the right individuals
- Set clear guidelines on the empowerments made
- Educate on the empowerments and authorities provided
- Provide required clarifications on empowerment made
- Advice on what to be done on expectations and define the communication paths
- Revalidate to ensure the provided empowerments are clear
- Closely monitor the outcomes of the empowerment on a continuous basis
- Guide as needed to ensure the empowerments achieve expected outcomes
- Reassess for shortcomings and take corrective measures on a timely manner
- Always grant empowerment in a gradual manner
- Apply lessons learned without delays in finetuning empowerments
- Provide sufficient time for the individuals to get used to the empowerments
- Have risk mitigations in place for potential errors made during initial phase
- Gradually step out from a close monitoring when things start to move smoothly

3. Leadership

3.2.4.5. Motivation and Recognition

Motivation and recognition are two things that are tightly coupled. Motivation leads to recognition, and recognition leads to more motivation.

Motivation is something that a leader or manager needs to do often. Employees tend to become easily de-motivated due to various factors and incidents that occur on the job.

Continuous motivation is an act that can boost employee morale. As a leader or manager, you need to make sure that you are aware of the employee mindset. You should become good at identifying when they are disheartened or motivation levels have drained.

While some employees may be open to discussing such issues, many of them may not be courageous enough to come and speak to you about it. Therefore, as a successful leader, one of your core duties should be to create an environment where employees can simply talk to you about their problems and what keeps them de-motivated. These conversations need to be kept confidential, and you need to maintain a good level of patience and empathy to understand the real problem. Employees expect you to be able to help in finding a solution, although at times, it will be quite complex to come up with a solution off the cuff. In such scenarios, you need to let the employees know that a solution is being worked on, and they will be informed shortly. Always avoid further de-motivating the employee as this will only worsen the situation.

Recognition, on the other hand, is something that you can practice as a remedy for any de-motivation. There can be instances where employees are de-motivated because they are not given the required recognition for their efforts or someone else is being rewarded for their work. Both situations could cause serious levels of disappointments in employees and could emotionally break them down. Therefore, you must minimize such situations within your organizations to keep your employees motivated to produce the best outcomes they can.

While sometimes employees have no choice other than to accept a task assigned, the quality of the output in such situations could have serious gaps. De-motivated employees do no good for the organization or themselves. They are frustrated and unhappy, and they will never give a hundred percent to their job. While there are many ways to improve the quality of their work, they have no motivation to look for them. They may complete the task, but it will be an average outcome or below, just enough to call it done. Elements such as passion and creativity are completely missing. Since the task is done to the minimum expectations, there is nothing you can do.

However, this case can be quite the opposite when employees are motivated, simply because they have a drive that always pushes them to do better than the minimum requirements. They always look for ways to improve, and they may also come up with innovative ideas. As discussed in the above section, employees can be self-motivated if you provide the right incentive and recognition.

As a leader or manager, you should learn to become effective at delegation. To achieve this, here are some things you can practice to make sure your employees are motivated.

Constant open communication will bring you the required inputs to figure out their motivational levels. Furthermore, you need to keep a close eye to see if they gain the required recognition for what they do.

Once you address the above factors, you will begin to see employees giving their best efforts to their delegated tasks and their output levels gradually improving. This will be a systemic improvement that will be gradual over a period.

The key takeaway from this section is that effective motivation and recognition will help you unleash the fullest potential of your employees, and in turn, it will help you effectively achieve your overall organizational goals.

3. Leadership

3.2.4.5.1. How to Improve Motivation and Recognition

Identify the potential demotivations within the teams over a period of time	Analyze the root cause for the potential demotivational aspects	Segregate the demotivation aspects within your scope and outside
Speak to employees to identify if the assumptions you made are correct	Incorporate employee feedback into your search for solutions	Try to fix the root cause of demotivations as the first step
Have a clear idea of the strengths and weaknesses of the team	Skip hierarchy when having conversations and talk to all levels of employees	Appreciate employees in a timely manner for outstanding performance
Provide recognition for employees who deserve it	Continuously motivate and build the moral of the team on a periodic basis	Motivate on failures and provide emotional support to do better next time
Allocate budgets for recognition and include financial benefits	Keep the motivation and recognition process both formal and informal	Ensure that employees do not take credit for others' work
Always obtain feedback on recognitions	Avoid preconceived perceptions about employees when it comes to recognition	Always make hard work the path to success and avoid favoritism

3.2.4.6. Respect and Integrity

Respect and integrity are two key areas for leaders. Humans by nature crave respect, whether at work or outside of it.

When you give respect, in turn, you will earn respect. When you work with your employees, you must always give them the respect they deserve. It needs to be unconditional, no matter where they stand on the organizational hierarchy.

It is very important that communication is always respectful. Always remember that only respectful communication with your employees will earn you respect. Only when you are respected will they look up to you and happily follow your instructions. Frustrated employees who hate their bosses have always caused damage to their organizations, and organizations with unhappy employees are never successful in achieving great outcomes.

On the other hand, integrity is something a leader must have in their character. If your integrity is questioned, that will surely lead to a situation where your employees will lose their trust and respect for you. Once those things are lost, it will be an uphill battle to get your subordinates to believe in you or follow your instructions. They will begin to consider you as untrustworthy and will not take your words seriously.

This is an incredibly challenging situation for a manager because when your employees turn against you, you cannot be a successful leader. Therefore, you need to be mindful of your integrity, and you need to work in a manner that maintains employee trust.

While leaders delegate tasks to their employees, it is important to ensure such delegated tasks meet expectations. If you are respectful of your employees, they will tend to treat your instructions with respect. Furthermore, they will always achieve the best result because they do not want to disappoint their leader.

If they do not respect you, the result could be quite different. The employees may complete their tasks, but they will not put in the effort to do them well. They will not mind you being disappointed because they have no respect for you and don't trust your feelings toward them.

3. Leadership

As we discussed above, respect is a two-way street. Leaders need to respect employees, and in turn, that will earn the respect of the employees. It is always best to start this cycle from the top down because generally, employees start out with a certain amount of respect for their leaders, due to the hierarchy in organizations.

On the other hand, integrity also plays an important part in delegation. Employees tend to like leaders whom they can trust. It is an emotional bonding where employees do not want to disappoint a leader or manager whom they feel is trustworthy. They will go the extra mile to ensure that they do their best for their managers or the leaders they trust.

While the commanding approach can bring results, it is ineffective in bringing the best out of employees. However, respecting your employees and maintaining your integrity can effect more positive results and higher efficiency levels. Your employees will be self-motivated and will have a passion for delivering the best to the organization. It will be extremely easy to get desired outcomes from such employees, and they tend to perform even better than they are expected to. This will make your job much easier simply because you will not have to pressure employees for sound quality or timely delivery. These things will happen automatically and effortlessly.

Therefore, as an organization, it allows leapfrogging growth as most employees will tend to perform to the best of their abilities. This is a win-win situation for both employees and employers and will eventually help you grow within your organization as a successful leader or manager.

3.2.4.6.1. How to Improve Respect and Integrity

- Use pleasant language to address employees at all times
- Avoid taking out your frustrations on employees
- Don't let anger control your conversations with employees
- Speak objectively and keep conversations meaningful
- Respect the emotions of employees in sensitive conversations
- Maintain the trust of employees by keeping your word
- Avoid creating a bad impression in the minds of employees
- Always try to become a solution provider
- Speak positively before highlighting negatives
- Avoid speaking to employees when you have lost control of your emotions
- Pay attention to employees and make them feel they are important
- Avoid a commanding style of work and be respectful when giving instructions
- Be a role model to employees by walking the talk
- Be patient and calm when you handle stressful situations
- Avoid jumping to conclusions by hearing one side of a story
- Speak genuinely and passionately with employees
- Support employees in difficult situations and win their hearts as a leader
- Act mature and responsible and earn your employees' goodwill

3. Leadership

3.2.4.7. Avoiding Micromanagement

Micromanagement is a management style that results in managers or leaders being involved in every detail of an employee's work. It has disadvantages both for the supervisor and for the employee.

From a leader/manager's standpoint, micromanagement is very time-consuming, which means they will not be very efficient in doing their own jobs as they are preoccupied with the petty tasks the junior level staff need to focus on.

If this is practiced for a long time, it may result in situations where junior employees become dependent on their managers, and they will gradually relinquish ownership of their work since the manager is controlling it anyway. This could also be a roadblock for employees as everything needs to be channeled via the leader.

This also causes employees to be less confident about themselves. They will learn not to trust their own judgment or skills and they will always have the feeling that management is not happy with their work, since there is always something that should have been done differently. This is very damaging to the employee's morale, and their self-esteem will suffer. They begin to feel incapable, and this invariably drains their motivation levels too.

In an overall sense, micromanagement always causes more harm than benefit. Therefore, it is essential for leaders to managers to avoid this strategy. However, this does not mean that management should not double-check the employees' work. There need to be some milestone checks at a high level to see if it is meeting the quality standards.

Employees need a sense of freedom. Feeling like they are being watched at every step results in an unfavorable work condition where employees will be frustrated and demotivated.

Delegating in a micromanaged environment are less effective as well as both employees and managers are at their lowest efficiency levels.

If you wish to become a successful leader, stay away from micromanaging your employees. If you have had this tendency in the past, it may be a little challenging to drop it all at once. You may need to take a step-by-step approach to change your management style. Begin by coming up with milestones where you can do a quick check to make sure that things are moving well. Once you do this over a while, you will slowly start building up your team's confidence. When this is improving, you can further reduce your direct involvement in their tasks. Gradual milestone monitoring can start at a day-end process to move gradually to every two days, then weekly, monthly, and quarterly.

Once you start to avoid micromanagement, you will gradually see the confidence and moral levels of teams increase, and you can start using effective feedback processes that allow your employees to express how the gradual changes are affecting their workplace freedom and happiness.

3.2.4.7.1. How to Improve on Avoiding Micromanagement

Identify the root cause for the need of microman-agement	Take corrective actions to fix root causes for microman-agement	Identify employees and do an effective delegation of tasks
Create multiple layers of delegation for effective tracking of tasks	Identify employee skill gaps and fix them to ensure improved capabilities	Identify potential risks associated with delegation and take corrective measures to address them
Run trial delegations and access outcomes on smaller engagements	Introduce checks and balances to ensure quality of outcomes	Have checkpoint meetings on a periodic basis and track at a high level
Identify potential outcome gaps due to delegation	Take corrective actions to address the delegation gaps in a timely manner	Keep communications simple and clear to avoid any ambiguity

3. Leadership

Give employees freedom to think and be creative	Obtain employee feedback and input on areas of improvements	Put your trust in employees and their capabilities
Monitor employees that require closer attention and support	Improve communications and interactions with employees	Invest in solutions for task tracking and monitoring

Chapter Two

4. Operations

4.1. What Is Operations

Operations are a vital part of business. All teams need to work together for effective operation. While business operations may vary, what matters the most is how well each team, from leaders to downwards, is aligned together in keeping the operations running of an organization. To simplify, this can be listed as activities the business engages in daily that result in some output which will help to increase the overall profitability of the organization.

These activities need to be optimized to ensure a smoother flow among the various departments, members, or teams who take part in the business activities. As leaders and managers, it will be your duty to ensure a seamless operation within the organization that ensures a productive and efficient output.

When mistakes or bottlenecks occur in one department within your organization, it can impact the other departments as well. The organization is like a big machine, and operations are the different components that are put together to make the whole thing run. Every department of your organization must continuously adjust to any changes required to achieve the overall organizational outcomes.

4. Operations

4.2. Key Areas of Focus for Operations

While there are many areas of focus for operations, our focus will be on the below-listed areas.

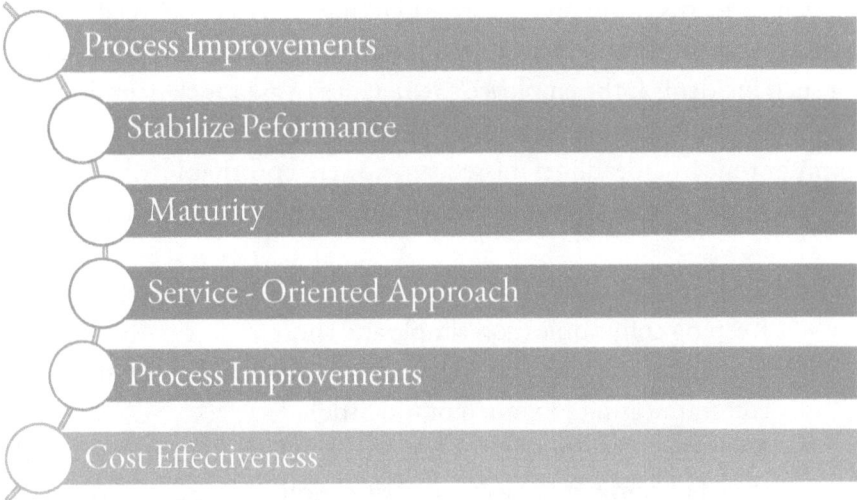

In the following chapters, we will be doing a deep dive into each of these areas.

4.2.1. Improve Productivity

4.2.1.1. Communication Gaps

Communication gaps are a common issue in most organizations and have a direct impact on productivity. A communication gap can be defined as a misunderstanding or partial understanding of a communication resulting in a full, partial, or minimal deviation of an output.

One common issue identified within organizations is that employees sometimes do things that deviate from the manager's expectations. However, when the root cause of such incidents is analyzed, it is found that often there was a simple gap in understanding between the person who assigned the task and the person who executed the task.

Some common reasons for such scenarios could be either the assigned person not paying enough attention to the supervisor's communication or that it lacked clarity and was ambiguous in nature. However, the results of such incidents could potentially lead to major gaps in deliverables, impacting both profitability and deadlines. Furthermore, one other cause for such incidents is the employee's reluctance to ask for clarification.

Finally, such communications gaps could cost an organization a lot in terms of time lost, deadlines missed, and lowered profitability.

Therefore, some recommended approaches to address such situations are as follows.

- Keeping communication simple and short
- Communicate only the relevant information for a task (avoid communicating too much or too little)
- Keep the communications interactive where the employee is allowed to comment or ask for clarification
- Request that the employee summarize their understanding of the task to ensure they have understood it clearly
- If there are gaps, help them understand in a polite and gentle manner
- Instruct the employee to reach out to you at any time if they require any further clarification
- Carry out interim checks on any given task to make sure that things are proceeding as expected
- Obtain feedback from employees on any confusion or inefficiency in the communication process

4. Operations

4.2.1.1.1. How to Minimize Communication Gaps

- Understand the employees and their communication abilities
- Create an environment where employees are free to express themselves
- Review the defined communication channels for bottlenecks
- Try to minimize the steps involved in a communication channel
- Identify the critical points where communication gaps could occur
- Keep discussions simple and easily understandable
- Remove any ambiguity from the communication
- Create an environment where employees can ask for clarification
- Always keep the communication going both ways
- Always obtain feedback from employees on their clarity
- Always encourage employees to clarify things rather than making assumptions
- Establish checkpoints to review the process
- If possible, carry out communications in the local language for blue-collar workers
- Enable FAQs for common questions to save time and effort
- Keep the clarification responses consistent throughout
- For identified communication gaps, take immediate action to rectify
- Share lessons learned on miscommunications for future reference
- Avoid making the same communication errors in the future

4.2.1.2. Roadblocks

Roadblocks, both internal and external, can occur in any organization. Internal roadblocks tend to be easier to address than external ones. They tend to have a direct impact on the organization's productivity levels by slowing down the overall organizational output that directly impacts organizational performance, output, and profitability.

As a leader or manager, it is your duty to ensure that none of your teams face any major roadblocks. While some of these situations are obvious, some of them are less so. Therefore, you must keep a close eye on the overall business processes for deviations and figure out the root cause.

Root cause analysis needs to be done very carefully because sometimes, the outer appearance of a problem may appear completely different from the actual root cause. Internal roadblocks could occur due to differences of opinions among teams or even among leaders. On the other hand, it could be due to employee groups or unions. For an optimum organizational output, seamless operations of business teams are essential. Therefore, as a leader or manager, you need to resolve such conflicts or disputes among teams so operations can resume and run smoothly.

For external roadblocks, there can be a limited capacity to resolve them if they are beyond the organizational scope. While you can do less about such roadblocks, you can always execute a plan B that will help you mitigate the majority of the risks.

The key takeaway on this section is that, as a leader or manager, you need to always keep a close eye on any potential roadblocks that could hamper your organizational performance and ensure that you address them in a timely manner.

Team-building activities can reduce friction among teams, and it can go a long way toward clearing up internal roadblocks. Furthermore, it is always beneficial to maintain good relationships with government and regulatory authorities and be proactive in taking required mitigation measures before a roadblock hits.

4. Operations

4.2.1.2.1. How to Minimize Roadblocks

Revisit and review existing processes to identify roadblocks	Classify the roadblocks as internal or external	Identify whether roadblocks are within your control
Identify the root cause for any roadblocks identified	Come up with a plan to fix the root causes based on their impact levels	Review past roadblocks that were fixed
If possible, try to replicate the lessons of the past to fix the current root causes	Brainstorm with the teams and key stakeholders for ideas	Think out of the box when it comes to identifying root cause fixes
Explore what your competition is doing to address similar challenges	Come up with a plan and put it into practice, then evaluate the success	If the output is not great, keep changing the process till it improves
Do not put off fixing bottlenecks	Always identify and document the impact of a roadblock	Be open for ideas from any employee irrespective of their level
Continuously assess the fixed root causes to measure effectiveness	Be open for change and adopt new ways of thinking	Document the lessons learned for future reference

4.2.1.3. Realistic Goals

Goals play a vital part in any organization, and the company's leadership is what drives the setting of goals. While market conditions demand that organizations adapt quickly to new environments and situations, it is essential that goals have the same flexibility. While goals should be ambitious, they also need to be realistic. Unrealistic goals will achieve nothing more than employee disappointment.

Those who set the goals need to understand the ground-level realities and the practical issues that all employees face. If goal-setting is done without considering the practical challenges, most of these goals will be unrealistic. They may appear extremely attractive on paper; however, they are far beyond achievability. As a leader or manager, you should first identify goals that are unrealistic and then take action to set realistic goals.

Any goals that require more time, skills, or talents than are available within the organization are unrealistic. Once you have identified them, the following are some steps that you can follow to turn them into realistic and achievable goals.

- Obtain feedback on the challenging aspects of the goal
- Analyze the aspects that require a change to stay more realistic and achievable
- Remove ambiguity
- Connect the goal to an outcome
- Include a timeframe
- Create an action plan for the goal
- Discuss the goals and obtain feedback before assigning

Unrealistic goals can make employees stressed and put them in a difficult situation. While achieving goals is quite important, it is also important to ensure that employees are given the opportunity to unleash their fullest potential. Therefore, setting realistic goals can be beneficial in maintaining employee happiness and effectiveness levels.

4. Operations

4.2.1.3.1. How to Improve on Setting Realistic Goal

Review existing organizations goals in a detailed process	Identify the practical challenges pertinent to the goals	Identify how qualitative the goals are in addition to being quantitative
Assess the sustainability elements of a goal in the long run	Take off the people dependability on organization-wide goals	Discuss with employees which aspects they feel need to improve
Assess if the goals are logical and if they align to overall strategy	Assess the S.M.A.R.T. aspects of the goals in a detailed manner	Involve experts with practical knowledge when the goals are being set
Obtain feedback from employees on the ground when finalizing goals	Have an idea of what competition does when it comes to goals	Have a plan B in place for if goals are not achieved
Always have checkpoints in between to assess the outcomes of the goals	Consider past lessons when it comes to defining newer or similar goals	Maintain a performance-driven culture
Avoid favoritism or bias when it comes to accessing outcomes	Take corrective actions immediately	Educate employees on the importance of goals

4.2.1.4. Skills Gaps

Employee skills levels can vary widely. While each employee has their own skill set, there can be many situations where you will see a skill gap. This is a quite common situation irrespective of the size of the organization.

While some employees might be open about their skills gaps, the opposite is more common. Many employees try to manage situations without exposing their weakness.

A simple and common example would be the effective usage of Microsoft Excel and formulas. While these can be amazingly simple skills, there are still possibilities within an organization where the employees are not aware of how to use a simple formula. If the employee does not want to admit that they are inexperienced in this, they could waste a lot of time trying to "wing it."

Skill gaps mainly drop efficiency levels, which in turn leads to a drop in overall organization efficiencies and productivity and finally profitability.

As a leader or manager, you need to have clear visibility on the skill requirements and gaps within the teams. Once such gaps are identified, you should put together a training plan to upskill the resources in the areas with gaps.

However, even though employees are put on a training plan, there may be times when for one reason or another, the training is not accomplished in a timely manner. There may even be some employees who do not learn the skills at all.

In this kind of situation, you should offer financial perks and promotions as a benefit of learning the new skills. This will motivate employees to give their best effort to the task. However, if some employees require more time or simply fail, you need to shuffle those employees to roles that do not require the skills to manage the overall organizational productivity and efficiency levels.

4. Operations

4.2.1.4.1. How to Minimize Skill Gaps

Understand the skill gaps that are pertinent withing the organization	Identify the root cause for the presence of skill gaps	Review the L & D process of the organization to identify any gaps
Come up with an organizational training strategy	Identify the skill shortages within the organization and fill as necessary	Make upskilling mandatory for all operational levels
Tie the organizational goals to the skills	Enable upskilling as a core piece when it comes to promotions and raises	Drive an initiative to provide financial incentives based on upskilling
Create clear growth paths	Enable mandatory cross-training wherever possible	Enable different leaning approaches for different user types
Make trainings more engaging and interesting for faster adoption	Enable elements of gamifications for development activities	Enable new technologies and tools for the use of the employees
Create awareness of how upskilling can fast-track career growth	Create an innovation-driven culture within organization	Reward and recognize those who put efforts into upskilling

4.2.1.5. Reduce Distractions

Workplace distractions could be anything that brings the employee attention away from what they do. It could be as simple as doors opening or people talking loudly.

Modern workplaces are designed to minimize workplace distractions as much as possible. However, there is always room for improvement. Distractions are always present to some degree whenever people are working in proximity to each other.

It is always good to talk to employees to identify the things that distract them from their work. You could also simply walk through the workplace and watch for things that get them to turn their heads or react.

Some of these distractions could be mitigated by changes to the floor layout, and some might require disciplinary actions.

With the current trend toward remote work, distractions could be in a whole new category. Some of the new normal workplace distractions could be endless email communications or chatting on platforms such as WhatsApp and within organizational communication and collaboration platforms. People working from home also have family, pets, and household chores that might be calling their attention away from work.

While these are new areas, they can easily lead to a lot of wasted time. Obviously, the more these distractions can be avoided, the more productivity can be achieved. Therefore, we highly recommend leaders and managers to identify and address any distractions within your organizations so that it will help you achieve the right level of efficiency and productivity.

4. Operations

4.2.1.5.1. How to Reduce Distractions

- Identify potential workplace distractions
- Analyze the root cause for such distractions
- Identify which aspects of change need to happen to minimize distractions
- Encourage employees to reduce unnecessary conversations within work hours
- Try to keep conversations mostly one on one and not as a group
- Write communications only to relevant users and do not copy unnecessarily
- Encourage silence within workplaces
- Keep distracting noises to the lowest possible level (i.e., ring tones, etc.)
- Always encourage group conversations to be held in private places
- Avoid using group chats to have conversations with just one person
- Try to minimize meetings as much as possible
- Evaluate organizational layout and floor designs to minimize distractions
- Always try to have teams working closely together
- Include as much relevant information as possible in conversation threads
- Have all relevant information on hand during conversations
- Discourage environments for office gossips and unwanted chats
- Try to limit the personal conversations withing organizational hours
- Leaders to walk the walk in doing all necessary steps to minimize distractions

4.2.1.6. Positive Reinforcement and Team Building

One of the best ways to motivate a team and produce incredible results is by using positive reinforcement. This means focusing less on what people are doing incorrectly and more on what they are doing right. By rewarding and praising your employees every time they do a great job, you will be able to condition them into doing well all the time.

While using positive reinforcement, you need to avoid favoritism. If one team member seems to be getting constant praise, the others will feel discouraged, and their morale and productivity will suffer. Try to focus on rewarding your team equally as much as possible. Also try not to overdo the positives. While people love to be appreciated, it will lose all meaning if you walk around saying "Great job!" for no reason.

Positive reinforcement is not a replacement for proper disciplinary actions in the workplace. It's important to focus on your team's positive accomplishments, but that does not mean ignoring inappropriate behavior. A great balance of positive reinforcement with leadership is what will create a good workplace.

4.2.1.6.1. How to Improve on Positive Reinforcement

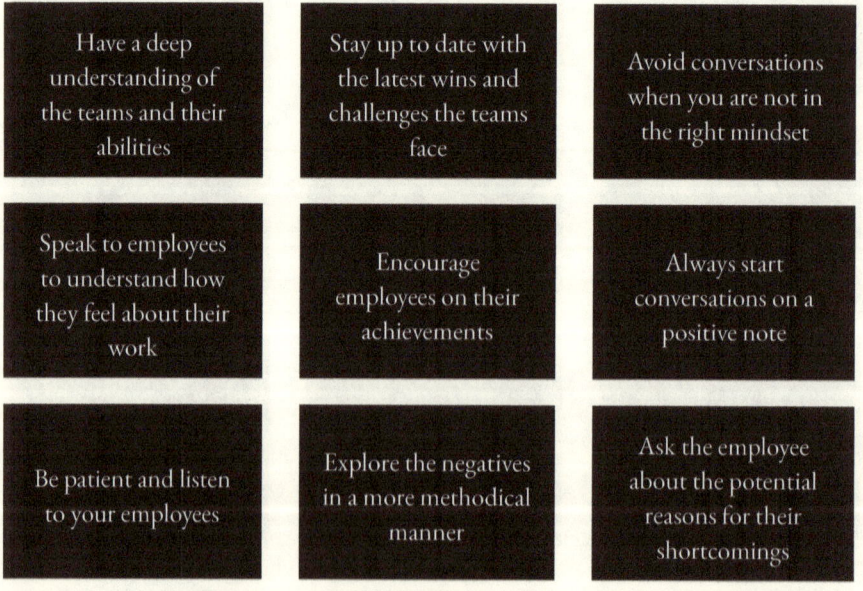

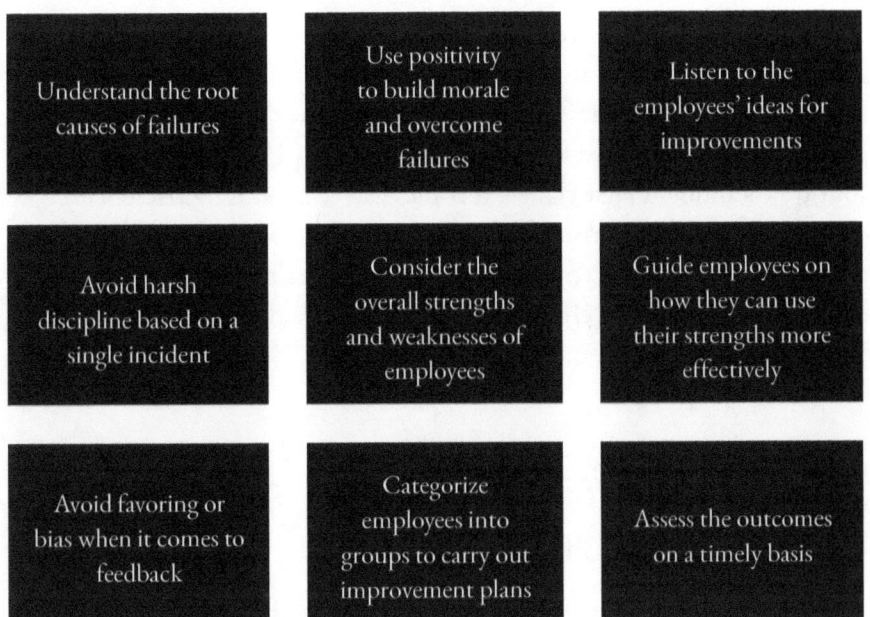

4.2.1.7. Improving Workplace Conditions

Workplace conditions are another factor that can have a direct impact on the productivity of an employee. Better workplace conditions raise employee morale, and in turn, produces better outcomes.

Workplace conditions could mean physical and psychological conditions too. Physical conditions could be a comfortable, pleasant and appealing environment that can help an employee feel cozy and relaxed. Even the design and colors of the workplace will impact employee outcomes.

While workplace conditions appear to be good at first glance, there can be situations where the employees are unhappy with certain things that bring their efficiency levels down. This could be loud noises or other distractions that make the employees lose their focus. Therefore, you must try to understand such potential challenges and ensure you address them.

On the other hand, there could be psychological conditions that may affect employees such as work pressure, team conflicts, and many other things, that drop employee productivity. Or due to a psychological condition, an employee may not like some physical structure or set up. They may have a fear of heights, and if they are made to sit close to the window, they could feel too stressed to work. While this kind of condition may sound ridiculous at first glance, it could lead to serious inefficiencies.

The key takeaway from this section is that, as a leader or manager, you need to make sure that your employees have a healthy work environment both physically and psychologically to make sure they can work in an efficient manner.

4.2.2. Stabilize Performance

4.2.2.1. Stabilize Challenges

The stabilization of challenges is an indication that an organization is achieving maturity. While challenges are unavoidable, stabilizing them means taking measures to ensure that they do not create a major impact on the business process or outcomes.

While all challenges are unique, one might seem to have a similarity to a previous challenge or something that a competitor has faced before. Organizational maturity is when the company establishes guidelines for actions to correct or mitigate some of the challenges they may encounter. They can be used as a guideline to take the first step toward a solution.

One such example could be guidelines for handling an emergency. In this case, the organization will have established emergency contacts for the employees to reach out to. The people in charge of the emergency handling will be trained to cover most emergencies, from employees becoming sick to a sudden building evacuation.

When organizations mature, they will generally have guidelines to address the majority of the issues that could potentially affect the organization's overall productivity.

As a leader, it is recommended that you focus on identifying ways to minimize the impacts of any potential destabilizing problems and work on a long-term plan to address them successfully.

4. Operations

4.2.2.1.1. How to Improve Stabilizing Challenges

- Identify the common challenges pertinent to the organization
- Identify the impacts of the challenges based on past situations
- Assess the frequency of the challenges and the root cause
- Take actions to minimize the impacts when problems occur
- Identify the risks and the mitigation strategy
- Document the process of how to handle identified challenges
- Take precautionary actions when there is a potential for challenges to occur
- Be prepared in advance for challenges and the likely impact
- Have a secondary plan ready in case the original plan does not work
- Involve subject matter experts when it comes to finding solutions
- Educate employees on how to recover from challenges
- Try to have potential workarounds in the event if the impact is under-assessed
- Consolidate all lessons for future use
- Train employees on a sustainable manner to withstand common challenges
- Classify the periodic and ad-hoc challenges to take appropriate action
- Use more experienced employees to work on challenging situations
- Be open for bold moves and trying things out of the box
- Consider the successes and failures as lessons for the future

4.2.2.2. Synchronization and Collaboration Challenges

Synchronization of teams is a very important aspect for any organization to achieve operational excellence. On the other hand, collaboration can be a major challenge to many organizations if employees are not getting along well.

Both synchronization and collaboration can work hand in hand where better collaboration can lead to greater synchronization. As a leader or manager, you have a major responsibility to make sure that you minimize any available synchronization or collaboration challenges that could occur among the teams.

Synchronization challenges could be identified as the issues that slow down an output due to the teams not understanding each other or not focusing on the bigger picture. On the other hand, collaboration issues slow down the outputs due to the teams not working well together. This could be situations such as two employees not getting along and having challenges working together.

For an organization to achieve operational excellence, it is very important to address such issues to ensure the operational inefficiencies are addressed. As a leader, you should always be mindful and keep a close eye on any potential synchronization issues among the teams. While some of these will be quite visible, others might not be. A close observation of the business processes and any potential delays could help you identify any potential synchronization or collaboration issues that may exist. However, when addressing them, you must listen to both sides before you make a decision.

Once the superficial reasons are addressed, you need to look at the root cause of the problem. While temporary measures could be shuffling team members around, this may not result in greater results. The ideal situation would be a root cause resolution, whether or not role shuffling is required. Once such a resolution is provided, it is good to continue to monitor the situation to ensure that the same problem or challenge is not repeated. If it occurs again, you may need to revisit your resolution to identify if any further improvements can be made.

4. Operations

While resolutions can bring results, employee attitude also contributes to a great extent in achieving the desired results of a resolution. While a majority of the problems can be resolved, employees also need to be flexible to compromise if necessary.

If any employee has an attitude that is disruptive and they seem to be unwilling to change, it might be for the best to replace that employee for the benefit of the company.

4.2.2.2.1. How to Minimize Synchronization and Collaboration Challenges

Identify the gaps and issues between teams	Educate the teams on the importance of synchronization and collaboration	Assess the root causes of synchronization and collaboration challenges
Identify short-term and long-term fixes	Work on team building activities to enable teams to better work together	Create more team-based goals and outcomes rather than individual ones
Emphasize the importance of teamwork and team achievement	Allocate budgets for team-building activities	Always hold the team rather than the individuals accountable when it comes to evaluations
Discourage a fault-finding environment among the teams	Try to identify internal team level conflicts if any persist	Allow different business teams to work together

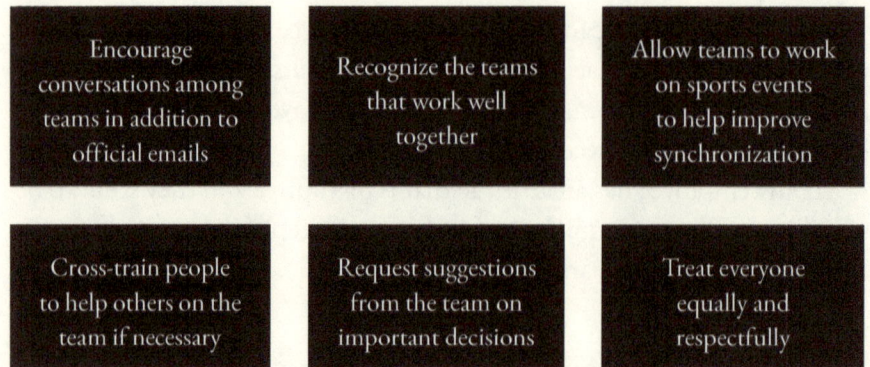

4.2.2.3. Operational Benchmarking & Excellence

Benchmarking is a way to assess quality, performance, and growth by analyzing the processes and procedures of competition or the market leaders. It can be done by identifying the key metrics that are relevant for the business processes in focus and assessing where your organization is currently at and where you want to be. Once the organization is clear on where it wishes to be, it needs to create an action plan to get there.

While an organization might be doing many things well, it is always recommended to have a higher benchmark to work toward doing things better.

One common type is internal benchmarking. This is a process where the business is compared against the historical data to see where it is heading. A common way to do this is comparing the year-to-year performance and seeing where the organization is compared to the previous year. This can be done with the different units, teams, or branches of an organization.

This method can be quite effective because, in general, employees within an organization face similar challenges and constraints. If one team can crack such issues more effectively than the others, that will be a good case study to share with the rest.

Competitive benchmarking means finding out what your competition does and setting up goals to achieve what your competition does. Such benchmarks could affect things such as employment tiers, salary bands, marketing to promotion, and many others.

4. Operations

When it comes to competitor benchmarking, it is very critical that you correctly identify your competition. If you do it incorrectly, you may find yourself with further challenges. For example, if you compare yourself to the market leader who is much larger than your company, you may not be able to obtain any useful information because the companies are in completely different places.

When it comes to quality management frameworks, there are plenty that you can follow.

4.2.2.4. Current vs Potential Gaps

Process gaps can be one other aspect that may have an impact on stabilizing your organizational performance. Process improvements are one key aspect that you can work on here.

Continuous process improvement is recommended for any organization irrespective of its size or scale.

Gap analysis is an exercise that you can perform on your existing processes to identify where they are compared to the process you wish to improve.

4.2.2.4.1. How to Manage Current vs Potential Gaps

4.2.2.5. Set up KPIs

A KPI is a key performance indicator, a measurable value that showcases how an individual or an organization is achieving the set key objectives. KPIs play a very important role when it comes to objectives or goal-settings. Any goal or objective that is set gets measured by a KPI.

It is important that you set KPIs in a manner where the objective is clear. Unclear or ambiguous KPIs make it very challenging to achieve success. Furthermore, you also need to review them with the stakeholders to ensure that they are realistic and practical. Setting impractical KPIs will only increase employee dissatisfaction levels.

4. Operations

KPIs should be actionable and easily traceable. While they are set as a one-time exercise, a leader or manager has to evaluate them over time and carry out any corrections on the KPIs to make sure they are actionable.

Maintain a positive attitude toward the employees who are open to sharing their feedback on their assigned KPIs. Such feedback may bring much useful insight that could help you setting more realistic and actionable KPIs in the future.

KPIs are tightly connected with the overall organizational goals and in turn have a major impact on the organizational profitability. Therefore, they play a very prominent role in your success as a manager or a leader and your overall organizational success.

Evaluating KPIs has to be done regularly. Making the duration shorter may give you more chances to make any corrections if the KPIs are not met. If you wait too long, there is not much that you will be able to do to correct any issue or problem.

4.2.2.5.1. How to Improve on Setting up KPIs

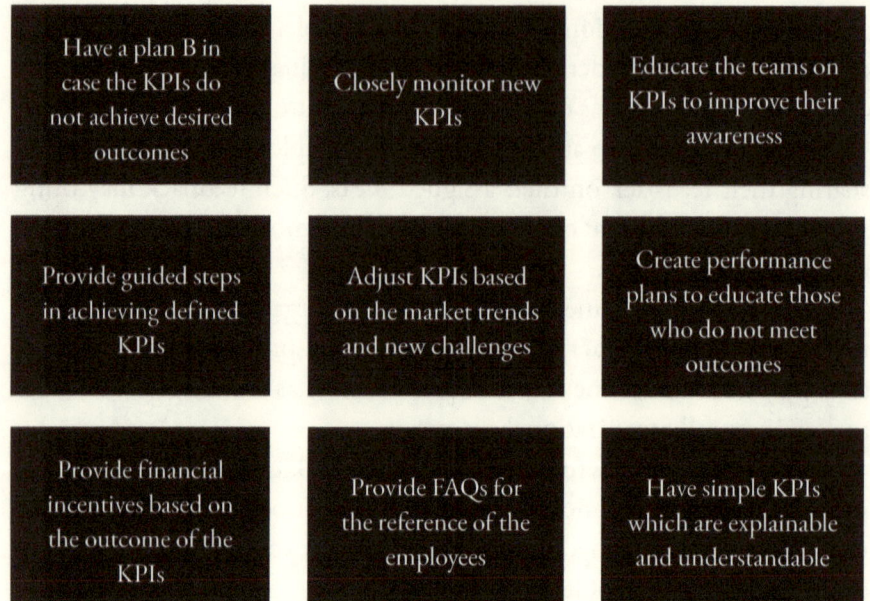

4.2.2.6. Sustainable Benchmarking

Sustainability is a crucial aspect of any organization. While organizations can have overly ambitious goals and plans, their sustainability is always a big question. Benchmarking is a way to assess quality, performance, and growth by analyzing your competition's and market leaders' process and procedures.

The benchmarking process can be done by identifying the key metrics that are relevant for the business processes in focus and assessing where your organization is currently at and where you want yourself to be. However, something that is more critical is to ensure any such benchmarks are sustainable.

Benchmarks should always drive the organization to sustainable growth. If not, they may have sudden hikes and drops in their development. These are not good indicators of growth and may cause concern about the organization's stability. It is better to have gradual growth that is sustained even if it is slow. Slow and steady growth is better than having sudden hikes and drops, as it may cause more significant damages to an organization's sustainability.

4. Operations

4.2.2.6.1. How to Improve on Sustainable Benchmarking

- Revisit the areas that require benchmarking
- Identify the benchmarking parameters
- Explore how competition is benchmarking themselves
- Identify the core areas of improvements
- Identify the resource and skill requirements required
- Procure the resources required
- Put together an upskilling plan
- Educate the users on the importance of the benchmarking initiatives
- Ensure that the organizational goals reflects the benchmarking
- Assess frequently to ensure that things are moving in the right direction
- Be open with employees to address their questions
- Carry out necessary awareness in the market about the benchmarking
- Work closely with teams to spread the word of mouth
- Take part in industry forums and highlight the standards followed
- Ensure the work output reflects the organizational benchmarking
- Ensure employee succession to sustain the standards
- Invest in employees and their well-being to maintain the benchmarking
- Revisit the benchmarks and do necessary changes on a periodic basis

4.2.3. Maturity

4.2.3.1. Challenges on Team Alignment and Collaboration

All organizations have challenges irrespective of their size or the nature of their business. However, when an organization reaches maturity, it should have come up with solutions for most of its problems. Furthermore, it will also have a standard process and guidelines in place to address common challenges.

One such challenge many organizations face is team alignment and collaboration. Since teams are comprised of individuals with various mindsets and attitudes, it can be very challenging to ensure they work well in collaboration. As a leader, it is your responsibility to identify challenges within the teams. To do this, you need to speak to your employees and listen to what they have to say.

Once such challenges are identified, you will need to take corrective measures to ensure the challenges are addressed. One thing that can help here is team building activities, which can improve team bonding.

4.2.3.1.1. How to Address Challenges on Team Alignment and Collaboration

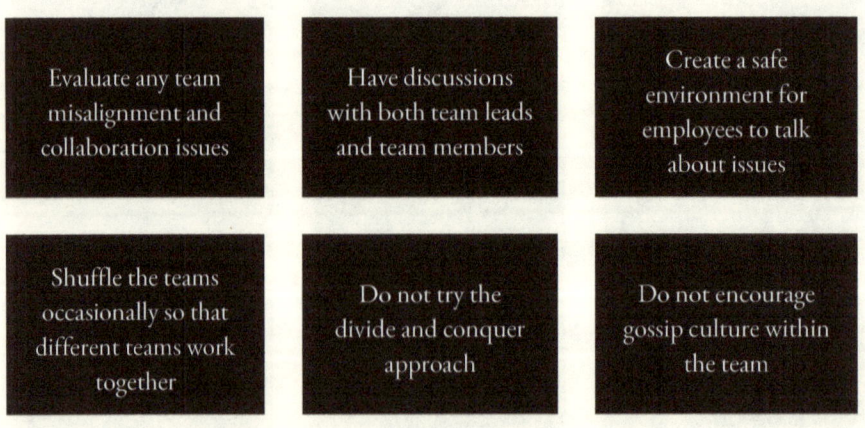

4. Operations

4.2.3.2. Lessons Learned

Lessons learned is one crucial area for any organization. It allows organizations to focus on what went well, what went badly, and what can be corrected.

When successes are identified, organizations need to make sure that they continue to do the same good things in the future. However, additional focus needs to be placed on the failures to decide what changes need to be made. As a leader or manager, it is your job to focus on those areas and develop an action plan on how to improve. These need to be tied up with individual KPIs of the employees.

4.2.3.2.1. How to Apply Lessons Learned

- Put a process in place to capture lessons learned
- Revisit the documented lessons on a periodic basis
- Carry out team discussions to identify the key lessons
- Brainstorm on how the key lessons could be applied
- Always look for past lessons when there are any challenges
- Explore the industry to identify how others have overcome challenges
- Assess and identify the impact of each lesson and the benefits it could bring
- Apply the lessons effectively and assess the outcomes
- Always document any new things attempted
- Classify the lessons into subject areas for future reference
- After each assignment, assess what went well and what didn't
- Assess how to do better on the areas that went well
- Assess what to improve on the areas which were not done so well
- Assess what to do differently for the areas which had failures
- Educate the teams on the importance on learning from experience
- Try to fail fast rather than failing late
- Ensure that you don't make the same mistake twice
- Be innovative in finding solutions and think outside the box

4.2.3.3. Revisiting the Business Model and Value Chains

Business models and value chains are not a static feature of an organization. They continually evolve based on business growth and strategic changes.

While businesses mature and develop their processes and operations, it is essential that leadership periodically revisits the business models and value chains to ensure that the required changes are on par with the evolving business nature.

There are some critical instances which more than ever call for a business model revisit. One case would be when the organization is planning to start a new product or a business line or firm up an already established business line or product. Another such situation could be when it is planning an expansion from a market or geographic standpoint. There are many factors to consider in such expansions. From a strategic standpoint, an organization needs to focus if the business model and the value chains are mapping well to make sure its business model will accommodate such changes and the strategies are well thought through.

Furthermore, one other important aspect which requires a deep analysis of the business model and value chains is when the business wants to turn around a company that is not doing well. This could be either a part of the total business operations or an acquired business.

This situation requires a strategic reevaluation of the business model and value chains to understand where things went wrong and to identify the root cause. After the corrections are made, it is essential for the business to reassess and analyze the business model and value chains to make sure they will produce the required results.

4.2.3.3.1. How to Improve on Revisiting the Business Model and Value Chains

Revisit the excising business model of the organization	Identify the areas of improvements which need to be made	Assess the value chains to ensure that it is comprehensive
Brainstorm with the key teams on how the business module could be improved	Assess to see if the past risks are still valid	Assess to evaluate if the risk mitigations in place are still valid with current context
Do the required changes on the revenue streams per market dynamics	Obtain opinion from the teams on the improvements required	Assess the key partners and validate if it's in order
Explore to see if the key resources are captured comprehensively	Assess if the business value proposition is captured accurately and still valid	Evaluate if the customer relationships are captured accurately
Identify any required improvements on the cost structure	Educate the key teams on the business model canvas and its importance	Evaluate improvements needed to stay aligned to organizational goals
Review the changes made and assess its relevance over a period	Correct any further changes as and when needed	Conduct a review at least every quarter to stay relevant

4.2.3.4. Out of the Box Thinking

Thinking out of the box is supposed to mean approaching problems in an atypical way. Such thinking involves much creativity and free- thought. Especially such thinkers need to withstand the business challenges they undergo and challenge the status quo.

Thinking outside the box means tackling an issue from a new angle. When it comes to innovation, this approach is essential.

Creative thinking, or the cognitive processes that result in innovative ideas and things, is often assumed to be predicated on thinking "beyond the box."

Creativity is assumed to require that we break away from our knowledge and use some extraordinary thought process to leap into the unknown.

This thinking is essential for organizations to achieve tremendous success in turbulent times.

As a leader or manager, there are many advantages to thinking out of the box. One of the key responsibilities of a manager is to anticipate and make changes to ensure that your organization is performing well. Leaders need to innovate continuously to achieve success. Thinking out of the box is about unlocking creativity.

As a Manager or leader, you need to step out of your comfort zone as you can not get to the next level by doing what you have always done. It will help if you are courageous enough to take challenges and try different things and to challenge the status quo. As a successful leader, you should be aware that whatever the problem or challenge you have, most or all of the time, the solutions are just there; it is a matter of finding them.

Finding the solution always requires you to step out of your comfort zone and put in additional effort.

4.2.3.4.1. How to Improve on Out of the Box Thinking

Identify the work place challenges faced by employees	Remove all possible mental stress elements faced by employees	Encourage employees to think creatively
Design workplaces in a manner which encourages creative thinking	Remove distractions from the work environment	Create a free-thinking workplace environment
Be open for conversations with employees	Be positive and encouraging toward ideas put forward by employees	Have continuous brainstorming sessions and idea generation events
Have a reward scheme in place for the best ideas brought forward	Implement ideas and assess their effectiveness over time	Take corrective actions to carry out any improvements on implemented ideas
Encourage employees to think differently	Encourage employees to see things from a different point of view	Avoid developing a culture of blame when ideas go wrong
Invest in activities that improve employee creativity	Drive innovating thought process within the organization	Be open for failures and look at them in a positive way

4. Operations

4.2.3.5. Challenging the Status Quo

The term *status quo* means the current state of affairs. Challenging the status quo means challenging the existing state of affairs at a workplace. It means asking why and trying to identify better ways of doing things.

Anyone can challenge the status quo. However, it is important to do it appropriately. As leaders and managers, it is essential that you create a suitable environment for your employees to challenge the status quo. If it seems to be discouraged, they will be afraid to do it.

Furthermore, as a successful leader or manager, the change needs to start with you. You must make sure that you are also unafraid to challenge the status quo. Once you do this, your employees will begin to follow your example.

Challenging the status quo takes bravery and involves risk-taking at a greater level. It also requires the ability to tolerate uncertainty. In a broader sense, challenging the status quo can be identified as getting comfortable with change.

Everyone has their comfort zones. Many employees and even leaders are often reluctant to step outside their comfort zones. It can be very challenging to think and act differently than you've done before, but it is necessary if you want to grow, which involves taking risks. No one has ever experienced growth by staying in their comfort zone.

If you are a successful leader, you need to be brave enough to take risks. Risk is what you are rewarded for. Therefore, you need to first step out of your comfort zone, and then encourage your employees to do the same. This will help you see things from a new perspective.

4.2.3.5.1. How to Improve on Challenging the Status Quo

- Question the existing status quo
- Question the purpose and the "Why" of the things you do
- Analyze the current processes to explore further the "Why" element
- Identify the mandatory and optional process points
- Be bold and open to trying things differently
- Be courageous enough to fail and try again
- Speak to experts to understand the potential impacts of introducing change
- Determine how to change the existing ways of doing things
- Closely monitor post changes to identify any potential roadblocks
- Encourage employees to challenge the status quo
- Create a positive environment which is open for change
- Encourage and be receptive to suggestions for change
- Encourage employees to step out of their comfort zones
- Encourage critical thinking and risk-taking
- Educate employees on the risk and reward models in challenging the status quo
- Be able to tolerate uncertainty
- Begin to see things from different perspectives
- Support employees in implementing change and be a change agent

4.2.3.6. Continuous Innovation

Continuous innovation is a concept where organizations adapt to the changing demands in the market by identifying new ways and more effective ways to do things.

Innovation is the key to survival. When innovation stops, a company begins to die. The world is evolving very quickly, and companies need to evolve with it. In today's world, what determines success is how innovative you are as an organization.

People always used to go for brands and companies with a history and significant presence in a given market. However, market dynamics have evolved and changed, and now people are impressed with innovation. This is why you can see start-ups disrupting bigger and more established organizations. Even companies of two or three people can revolutionize the world. It is simply a matter of how innovative they are.

You need to understand that innovation is a journey. There are no such thing as the end goal. As long as a company exists, it is in a race to evolve, and only as long as you continue to innovate will your company survive. The moment you stop, you will begin to fade away.

As a leader, you need to create a positive environment for change and innovation. It has to start with you. Unless you are innovative, your employees will not be, either.

In today's world, there are many business models and revenue streams that never existed before. The only reason for this is that someone took the courage to explore and innovate new business models. Companies that moved in first and made the most of the opportunities became the success stories that inspired the rest of the market to follow. What matters most is who does it first. Whoever gains the first-mover advantage will share a significant portion of the pie regarding revenue and returns. Keep innovating and encourage others to do so as well; this is the only secret key for survival.

4.2.3.6.1. How to Improve on Continuous Innovation

Release employees from overburdened workloads	Enable free time for employees to think beyond work	Create suitable environments for employees to come up with new ideas
Encourage an innovation-driven culture	Invest in programs that teach creative thinking	Have monthly meet-ups to discuss new ideas
Look at innovation as a journey	Allow opportunities for employees to present their thoughts	Begin to reward innovation
Put ideas into action without major delays	Always try to grab the first mover advantage	When an idea fails, look for a better one
Keep employees motivated	Drive innovation from a top-down approach	Encourage employees to upskill
Let employees choose their passion at work	Avoid pressurizing employees for outcomes	Make employees feel valuable and respected

4.2.4. A Service-Oriented Approach

4.2.4.1. Optimum Customer Satisfaction

Customer satisfaction is undoubtedly the key for the survival of any business. While it may sound like an easy task, maintaining high levels of customer satisfaction takes a lot of effort and energy.

Firstly, it is essential to understand that one common strategy may not always help keep its customers happy. This I because each customer is different. They have various expectations that may even contradict one another.

While one customer chooses your product or service for its prestige, another could be using it for its reliability, while still another person could consider it the cheapest option. The most important thing is to identify who your customers are. While the numbers of individual customers could be very high, there might be only a handful of customer personas, or customer types. While some customers only fit into one group, others might fit into several.

Once you have identified the typical personas, you need to come up with a strategy to handle each of them. Each strategy needs to focus on the fundamental value proposition that you offer that group. For example, if one set of customers chooses your brand for its exclusivity, you need to ensure you give them more reasons to believe that your brand is more exclusive than others.

While you are trying to improve the value propositions for each of these personas, it is also vital that you identify any aspect of dissatisfactions. They can also be grouped together for the simple reason that customers of a given persona are likely to behave in similar ways.

Once these dissatisfactions are identified, you need to work closely to ensure they are addressed promptly to ensure customer satisfaction. While maintaining optimum customer satisfaction is challenging, maintaining consistency is another essential factor.

Successful organizations have always mastered the art of maintaining optimum customer satisfaction with consistency, and that is what has turned them into successful organizations.

Constant communication and interaction with different customer groups is an essential part of understanding how customers feel about your business. Listening to their needs is a critical factor in accelerating growth. You need always to keep a close eye on your customers as this will determine how successful you and your business are.

4.2.4.1.1. How to Improve Optimum Customer Satisfaction

Review existing customer feedback	Collect feedback from prominent customers	Analyze the feedback to understand the gaps between output and expectations
Classify the gaps as simple, average, and complex	Work on the simple fixes with the core teams	Put an action plan in place to fix the average and the complex problems
Discuss with key teams how customer satisfaction could be improved	Identify the failures in delivering customer satisfaction	Fix root causes for the issues leading to gaps in customer satisfaction
Educate teams on how to improve customer satisfaction	Determine the right candidates for customer-facing roles	Maintain a consistent customer experience via all touch points
Invest in a CRM solution to maintain customer relationships	Educate teams to empathize with customers on their frustrations	Train employees to have higher patience levels in customer facing rolls

4. Operations

| Encourage teams to go the extra mile to support customers | Reward employees with high customer satisfaction ratings | Enable healthier conversations with customers and employees |

4.2.4.2. Service Levels

Service levels are a term you will hear in almost any business in the world. While service level benchmarks are very prevalent in the service industry, they are equally important to nearly every other business or industry.

A service level speaks about all the elements that are involved in performing a service for a business and the conditions of the service availability. However, the exact measurements related to the service levels may vary depending on the type of service provided, volume of work, quality of work, geographies, markers served, etc.

Unless service levels are defined, it will be a cumbersome task to measure and improve the service approach of any organization. Service levels will help all involved parties to understand the level and quality of service. It increases the clarity of how things are performed. Furthermore, it gives peace of mind both for the organization and for the customer, as both of them will set their expectations based on the defined service levels.

As a manager, you always need to ensure that your business has defined clear service levels. While this is very common among a business and its customers, many organizations also practice the same within departments too. This could simply mean how one department works with another department to achieve the overall service levels. If there are multiple departments involved in fulfilling a customer request, then it is essential to have an inter-organization service level and external service level defined for the customer.

In the bigger picture, if an inter-organization service level is breached, it is more likely that it will have a ripple effect on the overall service level that the organization is committed to providing its customers.

This also gives organizations an opportunity to quantify the delays or impacts due to a breach and work on a strategy for damage control at the customer level.

Furthermore, it gives a clear indication of the limitations and challenges that an organization has in achieving set objectives. As a leader, it will be your duty to ensure that you monitor and maintain the service levels with consistency for a better outcome overall.

4.2.4.2.1. How to Improve Service Levels

Analyze the current service level breaches	Evaluate the existing service levels to understand if they are achievable	Identify root causes for the service level breaches that have occurred
Identify the one-time versus recurring breaches	Focus on the recurring breaches as a high priority item	Find out if the identified root causes are accurate
Come up with ways to fix the service levels to avoid future breaches	Speak to customers to understand how these could be improved	Increase awareness among employees on why service levels are important
Explore for process improvement that could help expediate delays	Invest in a ticket management solution to effectively manage service levels	Define an effective mechanism to escalate service level breaches

4. Operations

4.2.4.3. Root Cause Resolutions

Root cause resolution, in simple terms, means fixing the root of a problem. You may have already experienced that both employees and customers come to you with problems. While it can be frustrating, it is a part of your job whether you like it or not. However, the most important thing you need to keep in mind is that problems may look a lot different on the surface than they actually are. Therefore, it is always necessary that you do your analysis and study to understand the root cause of any problem rather than just rushing to find solutions.

Root cause identification can be both challenging and time-consuming. Sometimes, the root cause alone can be a tied up to another problem as well. If any problem needs a long-term solution, it is always recommended to identify and fix its root cause.

When a problem is brought forward, your approach should always be to identifying the why. The more whys you find, the more clarity you obtain on the root causes.

Sometimes an employee may come to you and say they are not in a position to complete a task within a given timeline. The first thing that anyone would ask is "Why not?"

The first reason stated will give you the most immediate reason the employee is unable to complete the task. Typically, it may be something like the timeline is not sufficient for the amount of work that needs to be done. When you ask why the time is not sufficient, you will unearth facts about the workload and schedules of the employee.

The next level of the why may help you understand that the employee does not get enough support from their team members in completing their tasks, and that in turn leads to more tasks being allocated to the person. Finally, the reason for one employee not being able to deliver a task may be linked to another person not doing their job, which has indirectly impacted them.

In such a case, the permanent fix for such a problem would be to address the issues in teamwork where people do not complete their tasks, eventually leading to another person having to shoulder the burden of them.

However, if you typically address the issue in the standard way, you will simply extend the deadline. However, this same problem may come up again in another task, and so on and on. The solution of extending deadlines will at some point become impossible.

Therefore, irrespective of the nature or size of the issue, it is always recommended that you spend time identifying the root cause and then fixing it. This will take more time and effort than simply extending a deadline; however, it is worth doing as it will help solve that problem once and for all.

4.2.4.3.1. How to Improve on Root Cause Resolutions

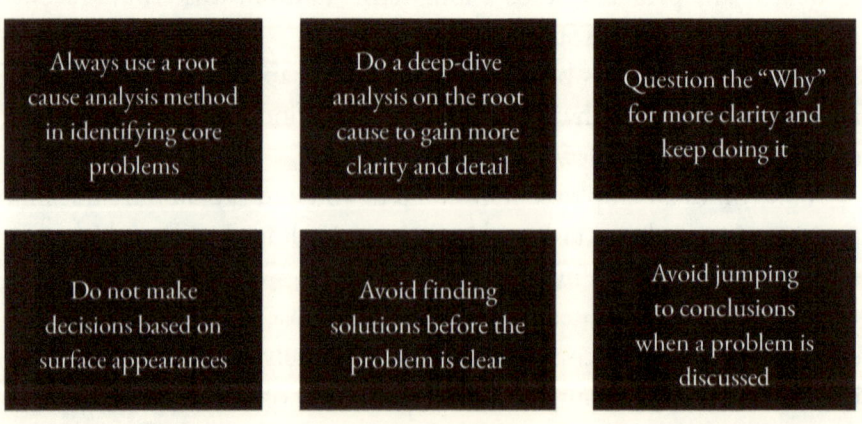

4. Operations

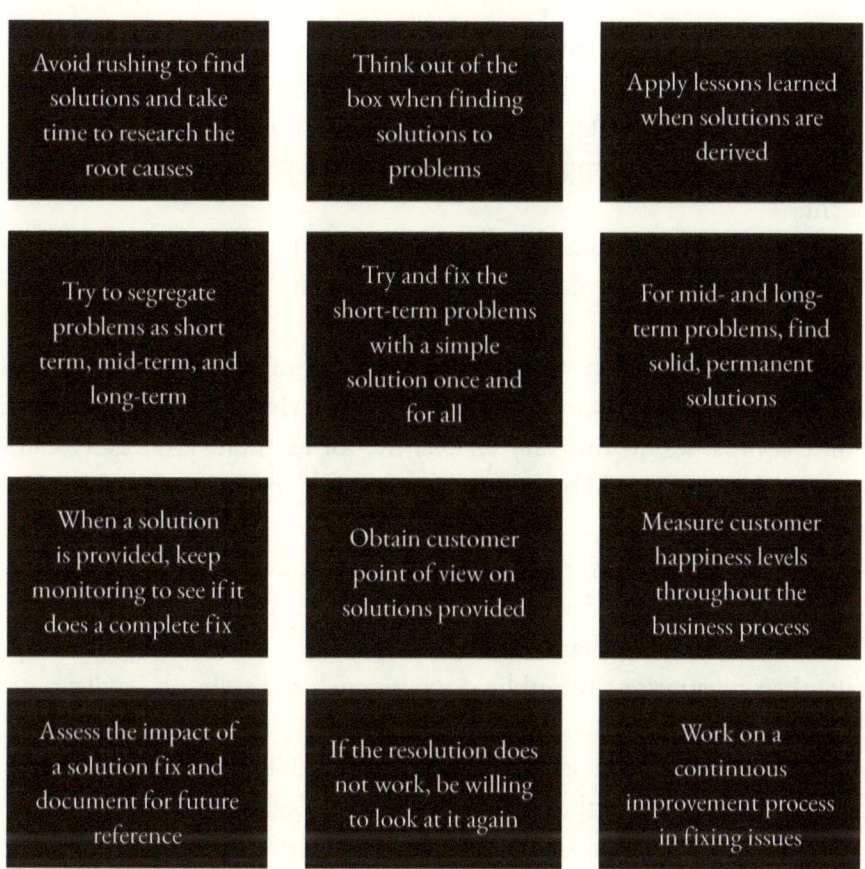

4.2.4.4. Customer Feedback

Customer feedback is one critical piece for any organization looking to improve its service to customers. Sometimes, the things we think our customers want may not be correct at all. This is a common case for many businesses. Customer feedback is a particularly important element any organization should focus on, irrespective of its size or scale.

Many times, when companies grow, they begin to neglect the customer feedback elements. They believe that their success is a reflection of doing what their customers expect.

Customer feedback may be very personal and unique based on each interaction the customer does with a business. Let's take the example of a call center, where a customer may be very happy about a service they received in one instance, but in another instance, they had a bad experience with one call center agent. From the customer's standpoint, they will rate the overall company as bad due to the performance of a single agent.

Furthermore, customers are quick to take up issues on social media, which could cause a lot of brand damage due to the fact that it can be seen by many.

To be successful in winning the hearts of customers, it is recommended that you capture feedback at an individual interaction level. Some companies do this very efficiently; for example, after every call, an automated SMS will be sent to the phone of the customer asking for their feedback.

Furthermore, it is recommended that you maintain a separate complaint line that is dedicated to customer feedback and complaints. This will make sure that customers can talk to someone before they take their frustrations to public domains such as Facebook, Twitter, or LinkedIn.

One common mistake that many organizations make is being inefficient in acting upon the feedback collected. Collecting feedback alone is not helpful if the company is not taking any action to address the issues identified. Once feedback is collected, organizations need to have a structured methodology for addressing key concerns. Once such concerns are addressed, there has to be constant updates to the relevant customers on the resolutions. Furthermore, the most important aspect is to ensure that the same mistake is not repeated because such cases may result in significant damage to the brand's goodwill.

As a leader or manager, you are responsible for ensuring that you have a very strong methodology in place for this entire feedback collection and corrective action process, and it is always recommended that you have a close observation of this process at least once a month to ensure things are moving along smoothly.

4. Operations

4.2.4.4.1. How to Improve on Customer Feedback

- Analyze the available customer feedback
- Understand the overall customer feedback across business functions
- Try to create customer personas and segregate the feedback accordingly
- Reach out to some of the customers to learn how to improve
- Try to identify potential trends and patterns in feedback
- Segregate one-time and periodic feedback quality fluctuations
- See the overall response rates vs feedback collections
- In the event the response rates are low, try changing the questions
- Make the feedback questions close-ended to be more specific
- Reward customers in some ways for providing feedback
- Have a process in place to immediately act on poor feedback
- Work with teams to understand the challenges they faced on poor feedback received
- Upskill and groom employees to better service customers
- Monitor over time for feedback improvements
- Try to create a best first impression for the customers
- Educate employees on how to improve customer satisfaction
- Closely monitor customer-facing touch points for any quality drops
- Try to invest in systems to monitor customer feedback more dynamically

4.2.4.5. Revisiting Service Levels

As discussed above, service levels are one important aspect of any business. However, one common mistake made by many organizations is not revisiting the service levels defined on a periodic basis.

This is essential for one simple reason: Changes in market dynamics are very fast. Service levels defined in the past may no longer be applicable. They need to be carefully evaluated and the required revisions need to be make to stay relevant with time.

While there are periodic changes to such service levels, there can also be instances where they need to adopt to a new normal market condition. One very relevant example could be the recent COVID-19 pandemic, which disrupted many organizations and their overall operations. In these kinds of cases, organizations need to be quick to make the required changes to their service levels to remain relevant in such challenging times. Service levels defined prior to COVID would not have been possible during or after COVID due to the numerous challenges aced by businesses.

There are many more examples, such as fire or damage that disrupted the normal cause of actions or the standard business flows. You always need to monitor for such situations and take the required actions as quickly as possible to make sure that service levels are revisited and amended.

One other important piece is communication with your customers. Once any change impacts the end consumer, you need to have an effective communication methodology to communicate it to your customer base. These communications can be challenging, especially if there are significant deviations from a customer's expectations. It is always recommended that you be honest and open with your customers to explain the real challenges you face. One-to-one communications are the best option to deal with some stakeholders. However, when situations improve, it is always recommended that you take the necessary steps in improving the service levels too, to stay in par with your competition and ensure you maintain your customer's satisfaction level.

4. Operations

4.2.4.5.1. How to Improve on Revisiting Service Levels

Evaluate the existing service levels	Deep dive to understand what could be challenging to achieve	Get an expert opinion on which aspect could be improved and how
Speak to employees on what they feel about the service levels	Speak to customers to understand if they feel the company is doing reasonably well	Decide on improvements to be done to the current processes
Re-engineer possible processes to fine-tune them	Train employees on how to be more efficient and effective	Obtain feedback from customers on aspects they wish to see improved
Train the employees continuously for effective ways of working	Upskill employees where needed for a faster response time	Invest in solutions that allow better traceability on service levels
Make changes to improve the overall customer experience	Think out of the box when it comes to improvements on service levels	Ensure effective escalations to keep the right visibility needed for breaches
Have multiple escalation levels based on severity	Carry out continuous, gradual improvements	Ensure overall service levels are sustainable in the long-run

4.2.4.6. Revisiting Benchmarks and KPIs

This section is quite relevant and continues the above section where we discussed revisiting service levels. Some changes may require completely new KPIs or benchmarks or an amendment to the existing Benchmarks or KPIs. In simple terms, all KPIs need to be revisited over time and in emergencies that require immediate attention. In a general sense, the rationale is that benchmarks and KPIs should also be dynamic and may be changed per the market conditions where it demands quick adoption.

Many organizations have a habit of a gradual improvement of KPIs and benchmarks over a period of time. This is for the simple reason that every year, the organization's targets keep increasing. However, it is also essential to understand that human scalability does not necessarily increase at the same pace. Therefore, impractical KPIs may result in employee frustration.

For this reason, organizations need to adopt different strategies to make sure the KPIs are changed in a practical and doable manner. Moving into automation is one avenue that organizations explore. Sophisticated software can help process things much faster with quicker turnaround times.

Another possibility is to focus on improving employee efficiency levels. This could vary from one employee to another as not everyone has the same capabilities for improvement. When revisiting benchmarks and KPIs, it is always recommended to classify the employees on how they have delivered their previously set KPIs. Then its recommended to do some level of customization of the KPIs and assign team goals. You will need to keep in mind individual strengths and weaknesses as you do this.

While two employees might do the same task with two different efficiency levels, it does not mean that one person is superior to the other. One might do better due to factors like experience, exposure, training, and also their innate ability to do things faster and efficiently. Furthermore, the personalities of people have a lot to do with their deliverables.

Therefore, it is always recommended that you pay close attention to people's personalities when you assign responsibilities. You should never neglect some employees and prioritize others. You simply channel the

4. Operations

right people for the right roles based on their strengths and weaknesses, and then you ensure you set the right KPIs and benchmarks that are practical for them and do the required customizations to ensure it stays on par with their strengths and avoid their weaknesses.

4.2.4.6.1. How to Improve on Revisiting Benchmarks and KPIs

Review the existing benchmarks of the company	Deep dive to understand their practically	Understand if the KPIs has a link and syncs well with benchmark goals
Review the KPIs and benchmark goals of the competition	Understand if it makes sense from a customer's point of view	Understand the priorities of the customer
Review and modify KPIs to reflect customer priorities	Educate employees on their contribution to achieving the set benchmarks	Improve team bonding and collaboration
Speak to employees on their feedback on the KPIs set	Review for the return on investment on set benchmarking	Change the benchmarking and KPIs as per market dynamics
Create awareness among employees on a continuous basis	Leaders should be able to explain them to employees without any ambiguity	Have variants of KPIs and benchmarks to cater to common market conditions

Be honest with customers in any shortcomings	Have deeper relationships with customers	Reward employees who deliver great outcomes on KPIs and set benchmarks

4.2.5. Process Improvements

4.2.5.1. Process Bottlenecks

Business process plays a vital role in any organization irrespective of its size or scale. Organizations with mature, proven processes operate more methodically than the rest.

Process bottlenecks are pretty familiar to any business process. These are the aspects that slow down the business process and its desired outcomes. The more process bottlenecks exist, the more inefficient the process outcomes.

As a leader or manager, you need to have an exceptionally good awareness of the typical process bottlenecks that your organization faces. They could be periodic or relevant to specific individuals or businesses. They can be internal or external.

It is always recommended that you do a quick audit or a random analysis of a business process to identify if it is delivering the outcomes in the most optimum way. In the event if you identify any inefficiencies, you need to do a deep dive to understand the possible causes.

In your deep dive, you may identify challenges pertinent to people business processes or even external factors. Any identified bottlenecks should be a high priority. The prioritization for fixing them depends entirely on how significant the business impact could be. However, any process bottlenecks should be fixed as soon as possible whether the impact is large or small.

4. Operations

4.2.5.1.1. How to Minimize Process Bottlenecks

- Review the existing processes to identify any potential bottlenecks
- Determine which improvements are possible
- Identify the root causes for the existing process bottlenecks
- Classify the bottlenecks as internal and external bottlenecks
- Classify the internal bottlenecks as minor, average, and major bottlenecks
- Identify areas that require process changes on re-engineering
- Review the current KPIs to see if they can be improved to address bottlenecks
- Discuss with the teams to understand any frictions among them
- Work on a long term plan for the average and major bottlenecks
- Identify and document the impact of bottlenecks on organization output
- Come up with process changes addressing possible bottlenecks
- Improve team synchronization and bonding
- Obtain support of process consultants to identify ways to navigate bottlenecks
- Set organizational goals around smoother process outputs
- Create awareness among employees on the end-to-end business process
- Work on identified process inefficiencies on a priority basis
- Come up with a strategy to address external bottlenecks
- Review the efficiency on the required process after changes are done

4.2.5.2. Removal of Non-value adding activities

Non-value adding activities are pretty prevalent in any business process. Reasons for it could be an organizational practice that everyone does without question, or it could be something that people are unaware of that is non-value adding.

When a business process audit is done, it is always recommended to be clear on the business objective and the desired outcome of each activity present in the flow. When some activity is identified with no apparent purpose or outcomes, it is always good to analyze why it is done.

You need to be cautious with this because one wrong conclusion could disrupt an entire business process. One such common situation is some non-value-adding activities that are done simply to be compliant to a statutory guidelines. Whenever a non-value activity is identified, you must involve all relevant stakeholders of that business process to justify why it is done. If it is removed, it has to be discussed and documented, and the SOPs need to be changed so that everyone has accepted it with full knowledge and understanding.

Furthermore, this should not be a one-time activity. It should be done periodically to ensure the business process is looked at closely to remove any non-value-adding activities. When the non-value adding activities are removed, there will be definite time and cost savings.

It is always recommended that you quantify the impact of saving such improvements to understand the true impact on the business. On the other hand, whenever a new process is created, it is good to go back to the common non-value adding activities to ensure that it does not contain any.

As a leader or manager, you need to have an open conversation at least quarterly highlighting the non-value adding activities that had got removed from the different business processes as a part of improving the awareness among all business stakeholders and department heads, so that it will also help them to revisit their process to remove the non-value adding areas.

4. Operations

4.2.5.2.1. How to Minimize Process Bottlenecks

- Review the existing processes to identify any potential bottlenecks
- Understand which improvements are possible
- Identify the root causes for the existing process bottlenecks
- Classify the bottlenecks as internal or external
- Classify the internal bottlenecks as minor, average, or major
- Identify areas that require process changes on re-engineering
- Review the current KPIs to see if they can be improved to address bottlenecks
- Discuss with the teams to understand any frictions among them
- Work on a long-term plan for the average and major bottlenecks
- Identify and document the impact of the bottlenecks
- Come up with process changes addressing some bottlenecks
- Improve team synchronization and bonding
- Obtain support of process consultants to identify ways to navigate bottlenecks
- Set organizational goals around smoother process outputs
- Set organizational goals around smoother process outputs
- Work on identified process inefficiencies on a priority basis
- Come up with a strategy to address external bottlenecks
- Review the overall efficiency upon finishing required process changes

4.2.5.3. Adopting Automation

In the current age of business, automation is one core area that any business should consider.

Automation is the key to scalability. While automation can be deployed in various ways, business leaders and managers need to look at it with an open mind. When a business process is analyzed, it is essential to keep in mind and look for potential candidates for automation. It could be simple or very complex, requiring sophisticated software or even robots. The key success is to figure out potential the return on investment automation could bring in.

While many things could be automated, it is always worthwhile to see if it makes sense from a commercial standpoint. Common candidates for automation are everyday, mundane activities that do not require much thinking or decision-making. They would typically require simple training in a tool or a method.

For example, if an employee does not know how to use some Excel functions that can help them do things faster, in this particular case, the investment for the automation is a short training for the person to learn how to do it.

This would typically cost nothing more than a few minutes of the employees' time. Likewise, this is a case-by-case activity that could vary from amazingly simple to very complex based on the effort and investment involved.

The key takeaway from this section is that you need to see things from an automation-friendly perspective. If you do so, there are very high chances that you could automate significant areas of operation that could help improve the outcomes of your business processes from both an efficiency and effectiveness standpoint.

4. Operations

4.2.5.3.1. How to Improve on Adopting Automation

Identify the potential areas qualifying for automation	Deep dive to understand why these are yet to be automated	Understand the benefit automation could bring to your organization
Review the frequency of the automation eligible process candidates	Come up with the cost of automation and the return on investment	Identify the skill gaps in moving on to automation
Identify the tools and technologies that could be used to automate things	Identify a period for a proof of concept of the automation areas	Work with process experts to decide on an automation strategy
Come up with an implementation plan for the identified automations	Obtain budgets and required resources to implement the automation changes	Obtain feedback from employees on their views on the automation
Obtain the buy-in of the employees on the automation journey	Remove employees' fear that automation is a job threat	Repurpose the time saved to some other value-adding task
Document the cost and quality savings of automation	Look for more and improved options of automation	Reward and recognize the champions of automation

4.2.5.4. Continuous Improvement

As discussed in the above sections, the business process requires continuous improvement based on business strategies or market conditions. This is particularly important to keep the business process relevant and stay on par with the market demands.

Continuous improvements may result in adding new steps to an existing process, removing some steps of an existing process, or completely revamping the existing business process. A total revamp might be in the form of a total process re-engineering too.

As a leader or manager, you need to always keep a close eye on the required improvements in your business processes. It is always recommended to identify any bottlenecks, remove non-value-adding activities, and seek potential routes of automation as explained in the above section.

This will be an ongoing activity that needs to be done throughout the business life cycle. It will never end for the simple reason that the external business factors keep changing. Unless continuous improvements are made, the business will soon become obsolete.

4.2.5.4.1. How to Work on Continuous Improvement

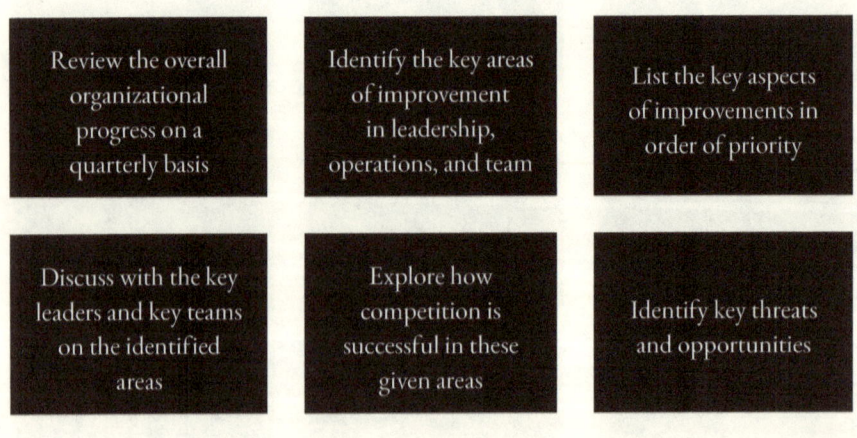

4. Operations

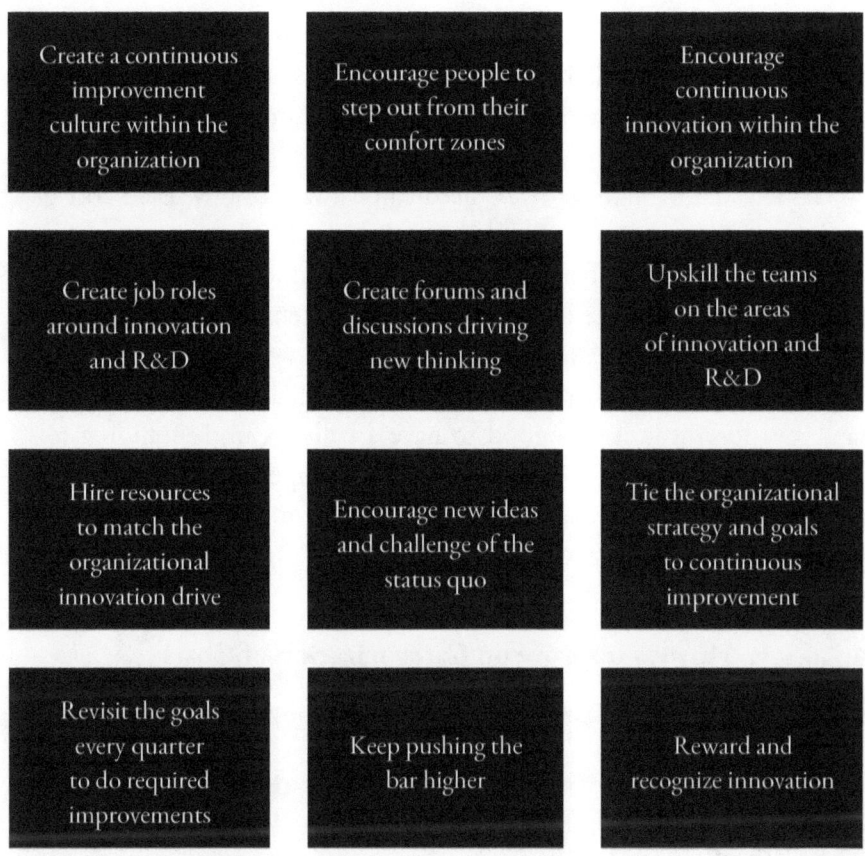

4.2.6. Cost Effectiveness

4.2.6.1. Categorization of Costs

Cost categorization is a significant area for any organization when running operations on a cost-effective basis. It means listing the different costs an organization incurs and categorizing them as mandatory or optional. Furthermore, it can be broken into recurring and one-time costs too. Cost classifications may vary from one organization to another.

Accurate classification of the costs will help organizations in optimizing the cost elements effectively.

Categorization of the costs may vary from a business strategy standpoint too. Some mandatory costs for a business at a given time may be considered optional due to a change in the business strategy down the line.

As a leader or manager, you need to be aware of how each cost of a business needs to be categorized in alignment with the existing business strategy. Furthermore, from an overall cost standpoint, you need to have a basic idea, and you need to be aware of the potential impacts of cutting the costs on specific areas to some level.

While you can obtain the support of dedicated finance teams for the same purpose, it is always good to have a ballpark understanding for a quicker decision-making process. Once the proper classification of the costing is done, you will need to begin identifying the true cost, as explained in the following section.

4.2.6.1.1. How to Improve on Categorization of Costs

Identify the main cost components within the organization	Deep dive to understand the real purpose of these costs	Identify the mandatory and optional costs
Identify the impact of the cost toward the organizational P&L	Identify the return on investment of these costs	Categorize the costs under mandatory and optional
Under mandatory and optional, categorize based on priority	Under priority, categorize the costs based on the occurrences	Identify the recurrent and ad-hoc costs

4. Operations

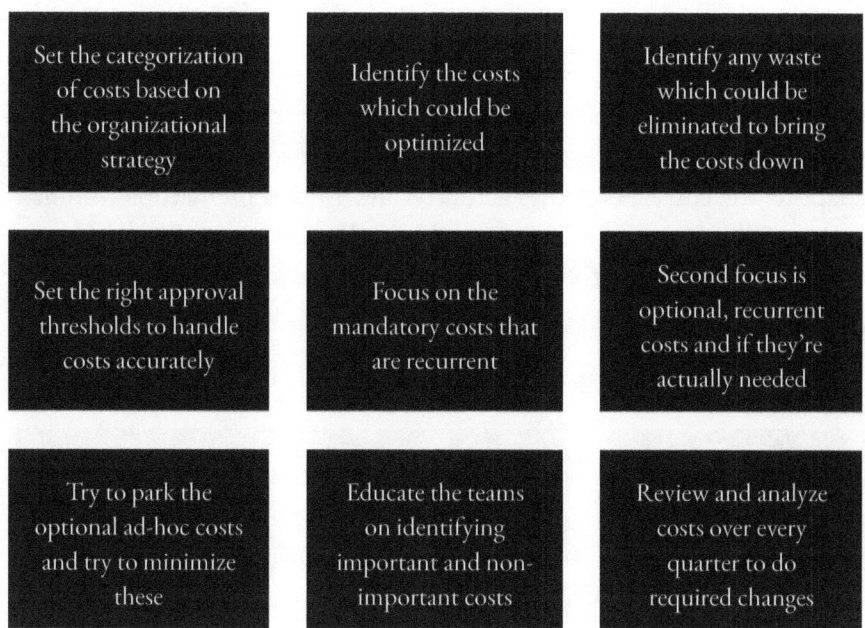

4.2.6.2. Identifying True Costs

Identifying the actual cost is very important in making any business decisions with cost-effectiveness. The true cost refers to the real cost required in getting the basics right to meet the business requirement.

When it comes to cost optimization, actual cost plays a significant role. This is because any optimization needed can only be made up to the point of the true cost of a product or service you sell. While businesses can have many buffers and risk factors factored in for a cost, there is always a bare minimum cost involved in any product or service. Unless this cost is incurred, the business will not have a way to sustain itself. Let us take a salary as an example. While employees are given various allowances and bonuses, there is always a mandatory base salary. Nevertheless, there is always a situation where a business can not go down further to a certain level. This may vary from business to business of any optimization. On the other hand, if it's a product company, there will be a base cost required to make the product, and no optimization can go further.

It is essential to identify the actual cost because you only know how far you have a scope for optimization. The scope of optimization may vary very much from one case to the other. Gradual cost optimization is always recommended for the simple reason that it takes some time for people to adapt to any cost change that is rolled out. If it is a premature optimization, employees may feel its impact drastically and could potentially lead to situations of dissatisfaction and even potential job exits too.

4.2.6.2.1. How to Improve on Identifying True Costs

- Identify the budgeted costs for cost items
- Analyze the actual cost incurred against the budgeted costs
- Review to understand the variance between the budgets and actual
- Review the procurement process of the organization
- Identify the points of improvement on the procurement process
- Distinguish the organizational views on cost vs quality
- Review the vendors whom the organization works with
- Explore other vendors to see if there is a significant cost difference
- Carry out a detailed internal audit on the costs incurred
- Work with vendors on bulk discounting processes
- Try to change the vendors periodically to give opportunity to others
- Avoid creating too much dependability on a single vendor

4. Operations

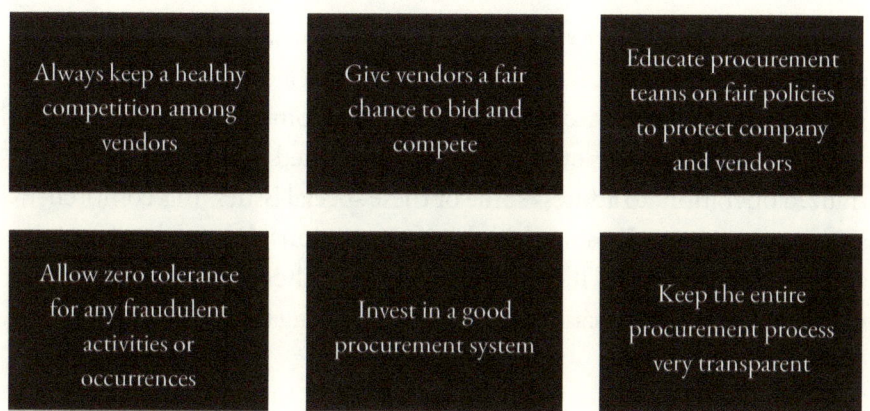

4.2.6.3. Consolidation of the Operations

Consolidation of operations is another avenue for cost optimization. It is also known as centralizing operations.

One key consideration should be how far some areas can be centralized when it comes to operations. While it has its benefits, it can have its drawbacks. While this is an avenue for cost optimization, it needs to be carefully implemented. If not, the centralization of operations could create many bottlenecks which will eventually lead to a total slowdown of operations.

A careful assessment is required when it comes to identifying which aspects of the business can be centralized. Some common areas for centralization are procurement, human resources, marketing and communications, payroll, etc. However, this strategy should be very much organization-centric. What worked for one organization may not always work well for others.

While centralization can help improve effectiveness, the effectiveness lies in how far the operations can be standardized. When standardization occurs, uniformity can be applied within the process, making it gain economies of scale. It is only then that centralizations will be able to achieve the desired results.

Furthermore, compliance is another critical part leaders and managers need to keep in mind when centralizing operations. Some operations require confidentiality and need to be done in separation from the others.

Such operations are never a key candidate for consolidation. While it can achieve economies of scale by getting it done via a centralized unit, it will be a breach of compliance from another standpoint.

Some organizations even go from a centralized operation to a de-centralized operation, to address some of these special issues. In a comprehensive sense, organizations need to classify operations that can be effectively addressed centrally, and if there are any outliers, these need to be addressed separately on a case-by-case basis rather than trying to generalize the entire operation.

4.2.6.3.1. How to Improve on Consolidation of Operations

- Understand how different teams work together in operations
- Deep dive to understand the potential synergies and collaborations
- Identify any duplications of tasks that occur within the process
- Explore areas on how a de-duplication of tasks could take place
- Identify the elements of waste on a process and see how it could be minimized
- Explore how teams could be cross-trained
- Explore the skill gaps that exist among the teams
- Invest in upskilling the teams to work in collaboration
- Have a strong governance process in place to manage larger teams
- Try to centralize the operations that could cater to multiple teams
- Try to reuse resources effectively in the centralization process
- Work closely on the teething issues during centralization

4. Operations

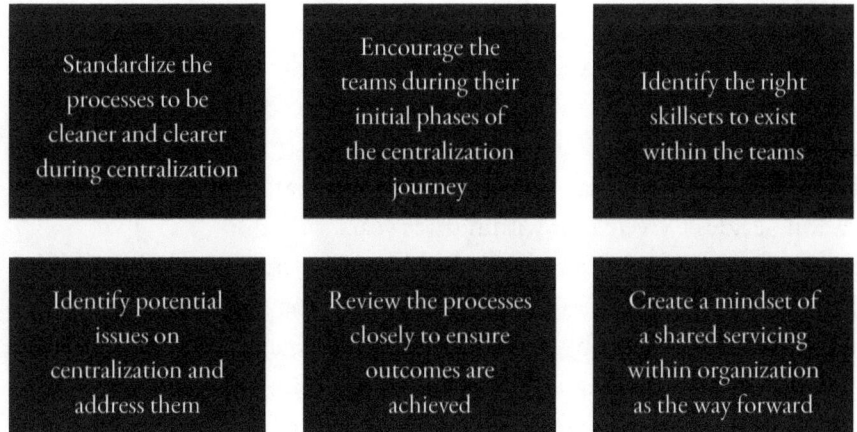

4.2.6.4. Return on Investment

While cost is an expense that needs to be incurred, an investment is a cost you incur that will, in turn, give you a return. In simple terms, a business needs to be very mindful of where they spend their money.

While there are many types of costs, significant costs above a certain threshold need to be always looked at from a return on investment standpoint. This simply means that whenever the organization needs to incur such costs, they need to always calculate the return as well.

Generally, a recommended approach would be that all investments need to be backed by a proper business case that has the return on investment indicated very clearly for whatever investment is made. However, while this is good for any new expenses to be incurred, the same can also be applied for any existing expenses.

For existing expenses, the period of capitalization (if it is a tangible asset) needs to be considered when the ROI is calculated. Furthermore, a weighted scoring can be used in the decision-making process to ensure the proper scoring is given for any chosen solution that has the best ROI proven. If the ROI is not realized, the organization needs to have a strategy to recover. This means finding other ways or revenue streams to cover up or recover any returns not realized as per the planned ROI recovery.

While defining the ROI is a one-time thing, an organization can often change or expedite a ROI realization based on the business priorities. In some instances, an organization may need to recover a ROI before the agreed-upon initial period. For example, an investment is made on a piece of machinery. The initial recovery was for five years, but later, the organization decides to recover it within three years.

In such cases, organizations need to revisit their calculations on the ROI and make sure it is redone to expedite the realization. However, while the ROI can be planned and estimated, market conditions could impact any forecasted revenues. In such situations, it is always recommended to re- calibrate it to see if the current market contexts will stay relevant.

4.2.6.4.1. How to Improve on the Return on Investment

Identify the true cost of the investments made	Review to understand the actual, promised, and realized ROI	Identify the root cause for the gaps between actual and promised
Understand the causes for these root causes to occur	Identify potential areas of improvements to achieve promised ROI	Learn how the competition is handling the ROI
Choose carefully which investments to make	Assess the true potential before committing to any investment	Invest in a smaller scale and understand the growth potential before committing

4. Operations

4.2.6.5. Reusability

Re-usability is a commonly and widely used term in many organizations. Conceptually, it means trying to reuse or effectively use a company's resources as it significantly supports an organization in its cost-effectiveness initiatives. One straightforward example of this could be using the papers printed on a single side for any other tasks such as taking notes or some other useful purpose.

While it may sound like a very small saving or reuse of a resource, it may result in a lot of saving when done in larger quantities. Think of a situation of an organization that has 150,000 employees. In such cases, the organization could effectively save at least 150,000 sheets of paper if all of the employees use paper that is printed on one side to write down notes that are not very important or to be preserved. This can be related to any resource that can be used more than once.

On the other hand, another similar example could be the knowledge assets or templates. While this is a less common area, many organizations can effectively reuse many templates for various purposes. Let us assume there is some commonly used Excel or Word document that many employees use for expense submission. In such cases, practical usage of time and resources would be getting a person to invest some time creating a template that can be reused among many people, saving time.

Reusability does not necessarily mean reusing all available resources. While some things can be effectively reused, there are instances where reuse will not be the ideal option. It depends on the use case and the scenario. However, from a cost-effectiveness standpoint, it is recommended that the leaders consider encouraging the reuse of certain things as it can drastically improve spending.

4.2.6.5.1. How to Improve on Reusability

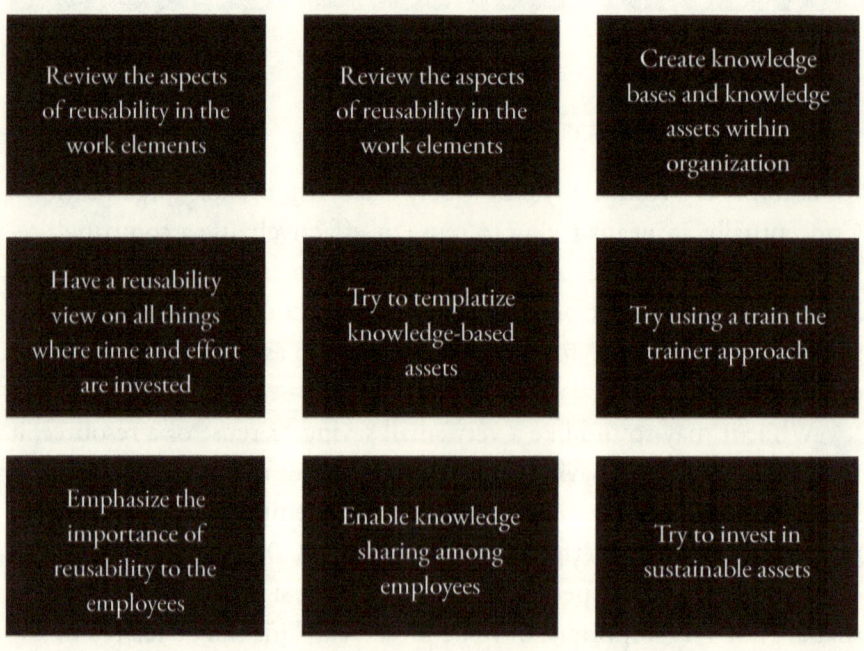

4. Operations

4.2.6.6. Cloud Adoption

Cloud adoption is another strategy that can help organizations spend much less money on their hardware and infrastructure. It can help organizations go from a CAPEX to OPEX model.

Generally, on the traditional operations, organizations are expected to spend money upfront on their computer hardware and specialized software. However, when organizations go to cloud, there will be subscription-based payments, which will be much less up front. It will even allow organizations to move into new technologies and solutions much faster as there are fewer barriers to entry.

However, moving to the cloud may have challenges for specific organizations from a data security and compliance standpoint if the data centers are located in other territories. In such situations, while it can be a financially viable option, it may not sound very efficient from a compliance standpoint.

While cloud adoption is one avenue for cost optimization and effectiveness, it is up to the organization to decide how far the cloud aligns with the business strategy.

One other advantage of moving it to the cloud is that hardware maintenance will not be an issue. Furthermore, the cost of protecting the data physically is also transferred to the cloud vendor. Backups for disaster recovery and many other aspects will be covered by the subscription fee that the organization pays.

Solution maintenance will also be effortless, from upgrades to updates, as everything is centrally managed on a remote basis. Furthermore, organizations do not need to hire skilled IT professionals. All maintenance is handed over to the cloud vendor, and the organization just needs to use their interface.

4.2.6.6.1. How to Improve on Cloud Adoption

Identify the application which could be moved to the cloud	Conduct a value comparison of the cloud for your business	Conduct a cost analysis of the in-house solution elements
Work with experts to plan for the cloud migration journey	Create awareness of what cloud migration means to company	Identify any skill gaps of the technical employees to adopt the cloud
Educate the leadership on the benefits cloud adoption could bring	Work with experts to understand the connectivity and any latencies involved	Come up with a cloud migration strategy with the support of experts
Choose the vendors to work with in the migration and platform support	Get the technical certifications done for the in-house support teams	Schedule the migrations on periods which the business is less busy

4. Operations

4.2.6.7. Going Paperless

Going paperless has been a concept that many organizations have adopted very successfully. While printing may sound like a small expense, there is a considerable cost associated with the printing hardware, consumables, electricity, and paper.

Today technology has evolved to a level where people can easily refer to content in a document or a phone screen, doing away with the requirement to print a document. There is so much unnecessary printing happening within an organization that can be easily discontinued. There are so many platforms that can enable collaborative working and accessibility to content across various devices and platforms, making the requirement of printed documents unnecessary to a large degree. Many solutions are integrated and connected across making processes like approvals, etc., that can take place on a platform, cutting down the need for a physical document to be present.

However, in some cases, a printed document is needed to comply with a statutory or legal requirement. In such cases, organizations have no choice but to print.

Going digital or going paperless is a journey, and it has to be a transformation. This cannot be achieved overnight. In the event your business is not paperless yet, the very first thing you need to do is to assess which business processes may not require a printed document. That will be the starting point of your journey. Once those are identified, you need to slowly evolve them, covering some easier processes at the beginning that may result from less impact even if something goes wrong.

The most complex, highest-risk items need to be taken last. By this time, with the experience in the other areas, the organization may have evolved to a level where the employees have already addressed the initial problems they faced on going paperless. By this time, all employees will be very comfortable with the paperless process, and rolling it out will be a breeze.

4.2.6.7.1. How to Improve on Going Paperless

Assess the usage of paper withing the organization	Identify the processes where the paper usage could be minimized	Assess for the processes where the paper usage could be cut down completely
Encourage teams not to print emails or documents unnecessarily	Have a tracking mechanism on who prints what and for what purpose	Educate the teams on software which could help read materials without printing
Look at systemizing the processes that involve too much paper	Keep a tracking mechanism for the paper usage of the organization	Minimize the usage of memos and other notices being put on notice boards
Minimize the usage of printed letters; instead encourage e-mails	Try using digital white boards and minimize the use of white paper boards	Encourage teams to make use of digital note pages or notes via mobile devices

4. Operations

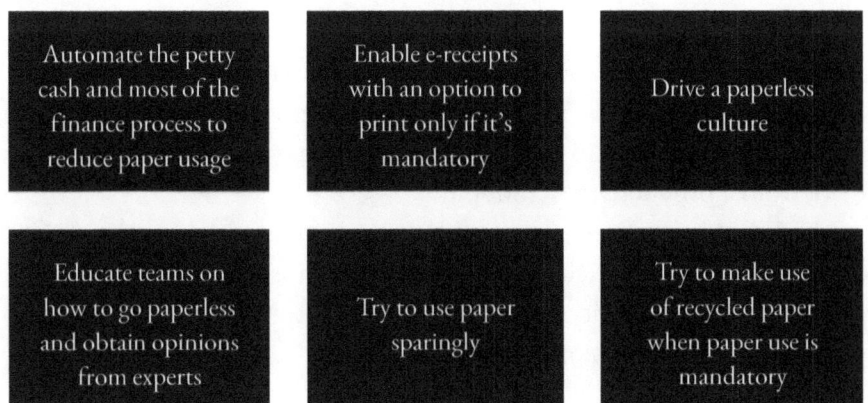

4.2.6.8. Remote Work Culture

With the new normal situation due to the pandemic, many organizations have started adopting a remote work culture. This has been a significant cost-saver for many. It saves on various overhead costs such as air conditioning, electricity, water, cleaning, coffee service, workspace, and many others. However, the usage of Internet and phone communication was rising. But even taking that into consideration, it is still a significantly cheaper option for organizations when the costs are compared.

However, it has some downsides too. Many employers believe that productivity rates are going down. Further, employees seemingly have less focus as they tend to get distracted with home chores and family. Remote work can only be successful if the employees have a positive outlook toward it and tend to be ethical in their work habits.

While some organizations have tools and technologies to track people's time on their PCs, it has come to feel like micromanagement. Giving your entire focus to work has to come as a discipline and not simply because the organization tracks what you do. On the other hand, even in physical work, there are situations where employees spend their time talking to their colleagues or taking coffee or smoking breaks. Even when employees are physically present at the office, they may still not be always productive.

A better approach to measuring the success of remote work is by ensuring the outcomes are met on time and reviewing if productivity levels are within the acceptable range. If not, quick actions need to be taken for the relevant employees in making them aware that they are not up to the mark from a productivity standpoint.

Unless this is corrected, it will lead to a situation where the overall organizational productivity levels are low. You must ensure the overall organizational productivity levels are maintained throughout for the organization to get their desired outputs.

4.2.6.8.1. How to Improve on Remote Work Culture

Identify the job roles for which remote working is possible	Enable remote working for all possible job roles	Validate if the organization has collaborative tools to enable remote work
Invest in tools that could enable smoother remote work	Upskill teams on the usage of tools for smoother remote work	Check the connectivity of the teams for smoother remote work
Enhance the data packages to the employees to support remote work	Educate teams on the trust elements of remote work	Emphasize availability and responsiveness for remote work
Avoid back-to-back meetings in remote work	Try to finish meetings a little earlier than scheduled to give people a break	Educate the teams on the safety and health concerns pertinent to remote work

4. Operations

4.2.6.9. Sustainable Energy

Many organizations are moving into sustainable energy these days. When it comes to sustainable energy, one central aspect is moving into solar energy. This is a perfect example of cost-effectiveness.

It does involve an initial investment for the equipment required for solar power generation. However, many organizations have developed a business case with an excellent ROI in the long term.

While there are many other alternatives, solar has been one area that is widely used across many organizations. Even though solar is attractive, it technically depends on your organization and its geographical location. If you are located in a region that does not have sunlight for a significant period of the year, then solar might not be the ideal option for you. But there are other sustainable energy sources such as wind, tidal, geothermal, biomass, and many more. The critical factor here is that organizations and their leadership must identify this as a potential area of cost-effectiveness. It will become a duty of leaders and managers to ensure the identified sustainable energy initiates are run.

While the ROI on some initiatives can be slower compared to the others, by and large, sustainable energy has been proven to be more cost-effective from a long-term standpoint than the non-sustainable energy that is widely used in a current context.

4.2.6.9.1. How to Improve on Sustainable Energy

Review the energy usage of the organization	Identify the mandatory energy usage of the organization	Identify the potential reduction or optimization of energy usage
Analyze the potential sustainable energy sources available	Conduct a cost benefit analysis to understand the return on investment	Make required funding allocations for the investments
Come up with an organizational strategy to migrate to sustainable energy	Work with external energy consultants in the transition journey	Find alternative sources of energy in case of periodic fluctuations
Work with government bodies to obtain required support in transition	Analyze the trends of energy consumption over a period	Identify any lack or shortage of energy requirements unfulfilled
Take a hybrid approach at least during the initial period	Maintain the sustainable energy sources in a timely manner	Educate teams on the importance on sustainable energy
Gradually adapt to use energy sparingly	Reinvest some of the savings of sustainable energy to expand facilities	Showcase this aspect to gain market attention and recognition

4.2.6.10. Setting KPIs Around Cost-Cutting

Last but not least, setting KPIs around cost-cutting initiatives is one of the most critically important things for an organization in cutting its costs. While many employees indicate a positivity when it comes to cost-cutting initiatives, things get only actioned when tied up with KPIs.

Cost-cutting KPIs may vary from one organization to another, and the responsibility of it may vary at different levels of the organizational hierarchy. As a leader or manager, it will be your duty to have a clear understanding of the bigger picture from an overall organizational standpoint. Unless the bigger picture is clear, it will become very challenging to drive such initiatives.

Once the organizational goal in cutting costs is identified, the next activity will be to identify the potential streams via where the initiatives need to be actioned. While some of the action items of such initiatives would be to cut down the total cost of certain expenditures, other action items would be around using the resources more effectively. Some initiatives may drive the effective reuse of resources, and some others could be like using cost-effective alternatives of specific resources. Therefore, as a leader or manager, you need to understand that your organization's KPIs around cost-effectiveness are unique. It would be best if you were careful in defining the right KPIs in driving adoption across organizations in these areas.

Since some of these KPIs could be very demanding, it can be frustrating for employees at the beginning. Generally, these cost-cutting initiatives are time-bound or done more aggressively only for a given time, especially when organizations are going through a tough time.

It is essentially the same thought process passed down to the employees at a lower level in the hierarchy to help them understand why it is essential for them to take part in such initiatives and achieve their KPIs and how they contribute to the overall survival of the organization.

Only when the purpose is made clear will employees be in a better position and mindset to give their entire cooperation in working toward the success of such KPIs. On the other hand, when the KPIs are not met, you need to take this a little more seriously and initiate some immediate actions. This is simply because letting go of these KPIs is not something an organization could afford as it directly impacts the overall organizational sustainability. Therefore, such KPIs need to be closely monitored to ensure they are met without any excuse.

4.2.6.10.1. How to Improve on Setting KPIs Around Cost-Cutting

Identify the potential areas of cost saving	Segregate the mandatory and optional costs	Revisit the organizational KPIs to see if they reflect these aspects
Set realistic goals on the cost-cutting initiatives	Make such initiatives periodic and sustainable	Avoid cutting down on important costs such as training and development
Educate teams on the importance of cost-cutting initiatives	Guide the teams on how they can support such initiatives	Add new KPIs if existing ones do not reflect cost-cutting aspects
Speak to experts and teams to identify the practicality of KPIs	Keep a close track on KPIs and take faster actions if not achieved	Educate teams on consequences of not meeting KPIs

4. Operations

- Try to enable more reusability of assets to enable resource optimization
- Try upskilling resources to be able to handle multiple skills
- Understand the root causes when KPIs are not met
- Obtain an expert opinion to fix the root cause issues on KPIs
- Make use of the savings for the long-term benefit of the organization
- Recognize and reward those who contributed toward the KPIs

Chapter Three

5. Team

5.1. What Is a Team

A team is a set of individuals who strive for the same goals. Teams play a crucial role in any organization. Organizations need to put special attention on managing teams effectively to achieve their desired outcomes. While teams are common within organizations, team nature, composition, and structure vary based on the organization size and nature.

Teams can have benefits and also challenges. As a leader or manager, your duty will be to manage your team effectively so outcomes can be achieved in a more effective and meaningful way.

Managing teams is an art, where it takes a lot of effort and energy to drive teams toward success. The most challenging part of a team is that it is comprised of unique individuals. Your duty is to bring all these individuals' focus to a common goal that needs to be achieved by the entire team. This can create challenges because everyone might have a different idea of how to achieve these goals. This could create differences of opinion and conflict within members of the team that could drastically impact the overall organizational performance and output.

In the following sections, we will look at more details on individual areas that are critical in maintaining and managing teams.

5.2. Key Areas of Focus for a Team

- Given below are some areas that are considered as part of the Team coaching.

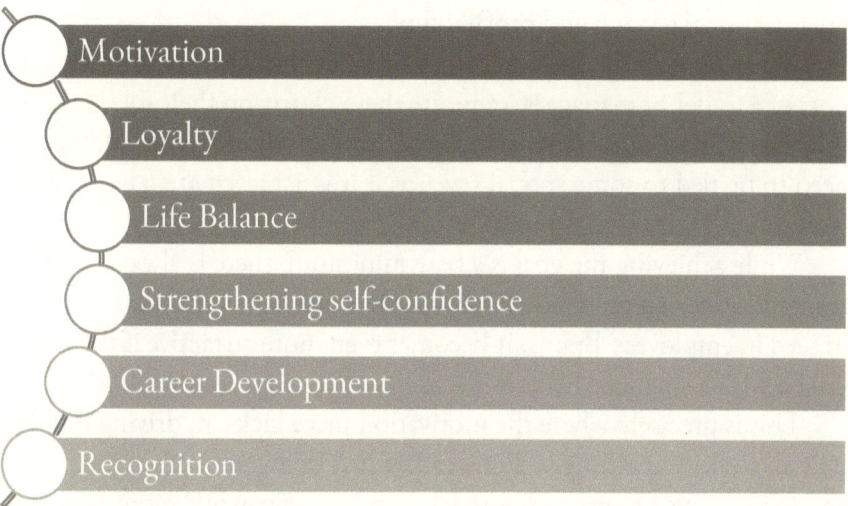

In the following chapters, we will be doing a deep dive into each of these areas to understand more about them.

5.2.1. Motivation

5.2.1.1. Awareness of Organization Goals & Targets

Every organization has its own goals and targets. Employees are constantly tasked with achieving the overall organization's goals. However, one main factor that could keep employee motivation at a higher level would be their awareness of the organizational goals and targets. If they are not aware of them, they will not be motivated to achieve them. Furthermore, unless they know what they are supposed to do, there is no hope of them doing what you need them to do.

One of your core duties is to make sure that you create awareness among the employees on the organization's goals and targets. Then you need to explain how each of them contributes to achieving the goals. There must be inclusiveness: The employees need to understand that they are part of a bigger goal, and their contributions matter for the overall organizational growth and profitability.

While some of the employees may be clear, many may require the support of a leader or manager to educate them clearly on their role and how they can achieve success. Furthermore, an individual's goals and targets need to be tied to some special rewards if it is achieved at an exceptional level.

While achieving the goal is a bare minimum, there is always a special recognition for an exceptional job, which is one key slogan that you need to seed in employees' brains. It becomes even more attractive if the goal is linked with a financial benefit if is achieved at an exceptional level.

This is precisely where the motivation piece kicks in, driving the employees to do something well instead of just doing an average job. Some employees may require support while others can work more independently. It all depends on the personalities of the employees. The key takeaway of this section is to make sure that you communicate and make the employees aware of the exceptions and the special recognitions to help them motivate themselves.

5. Team

5.2.1.1.1. How to Improve Awareness on Organization Goals and Targets

- Stay up to date on organizational strategic changes
- Ensure the goals and targets are always communicated top-down
- Explain the bigger picture of the goals and targets
- Create awareness on employee contributions to overall goals
- Ensure that successes are rewarded
- Reconsider the recognition framework when goals change
- Encourage employees to achieve their goals and targets
- Keep a positive tone when discussing targets and goals
- Identify the factors that hinder employee outputs
- Understand the challenges faced at the operational level
- Keep the hierarchy simple to make approachability easy and seamless
- Conduct timely reviews and provide feedback
- Work with employees in challenging times
- Make sure awards and recognitions are attractive
- Ensure that goals and targets are realistic and achievable
- Show inclusiveness of employees to the overall organizations' growth
- Remove any ambiguities in the recognition and rewards process
- Stick to reward and recognition commitments made

5.2.1.2. Delegation of Tasks

As a leader or manager, task delegation is one of the core areas of your day-to-day job. Effective delegation is more than a task—it could be called an art.

Delegation has a strong link to motivation. On its surface, this may appear to be a little confusing, but it starts with the fact that employees usually feel good if they are being chosen for some critical task.

This has to be done very carefully. You need to first have a very clear idea about your employees' key strengths and weaknesses. It is up to you to choose the right employee for the right task.

Once you have identified the right individual, you must make them aware of why they were chosen for this specific job. You need to stress the trust that the organization is placing on them to do this task.

This is when the employee will start to think about their importance to the organization. It will give them a reason to motivate themselves to ensure that they do not let down the organization or betray the trust the organization has in them.

Furthermore, before assigning a task, it is always good to understand the level of their interest in doing special tasks. While the thought of it might motivate some employees, other employees might have a different mindset. Some may even see it as too much responsibility and might not be interested in taking it on.

Therefore, it is always essential that work is delegated to an employee who shows interest rather than just thinking about who is capable. This may be a tricky situation in cases where there is only one employee for a given job. However, if you have more employees who are qualifying candidates, always make sure you consider their individual interest levels as this will help you achieve a better outcome.

5. Team

5.2.1.2.1. How to Improve on Delegation of Tasks

- Be clear on task priorities and importance
- Encourage delegation of tasks at each level top-down
- Ensure the communication gaps are addressed top-down
- Put a process in place to ensure the operational level is clear
- Speak to employees at all levels and obtain feedback on the clarity of the job
- Profile the users based on their skills and use this to make a decision
- Encourage open communication within organization
- Carry out periodic reviews to highlight issues early in the process
- Be open to discuss any practical challenges faced in delegation
- Try an iterative/step-by-step approach when it comes to issue resolution
- Recognize the employees who deliver best outcomes
- Encourage knowledge and success sharing among teams
- Use lessons learned as an important part on a final review of a task
- Avoid overloading people with parallel tasks
- Keep a clear line of command to ensure delegations originate from a single point
- Encourage teams throughout their process in completing an assigned task
- Creative positive competition among teams
- Keep improving the delegation process periodically

5.2.1.3. Showing Respect

All human beings desire respect. Irrespective of the hierarchy, we all feel special when we are respected, and showing respect is a key ingredient in achieving employee motivation.

As a leader or manager, you need to ensure that you always address your employees with due respect and use appropriate language. This can have a significant impact on their motivation and how they do their assigned jobs. It also needs to be part of the organization's culture for everyone to show respect to their fellow employees.

However, there can be situations where you are overcome by frustrations and begin to lose your cool. As a manager, you need to have control over your behavior. Even in challenging times, you should be able to rein in your emotions.

Showing respect is not only limited to what you say. In addition to verbal communication, you can show respect by your actions. For instance, when an employee needs support or guidance, giving priority to their requests is also a form of showing respect. Furthermore, when an employee is in grief or pain, allowing them to share their emotions is another form of showing respect to them and their feelings.

In simple terms, respect toward another employee or fellow human being is reflected in your overall behavior. It has nothing to do with anyone's ranking in the organization. Hierarchy is just a way to make sure the company runs smoothly, and respect should flow down as well as up.

You need to respect all employees and their emotions, irrespective of their level in the hierarchy, and to ensure that all employees are doing the same.

5. Team

5.2.1.3.1. How to Improve on Showing Respect

- Ensure that communication guidelines are defined
- Make respect part of the organizational culture
- Leadership needs to set the example with respectful conversations
- Respect should be important top-down and also bottom-up
- Educate employees on why they should be respectful to earn respect from others
- Educate employees on being respectful of people's emotions
- Discourage a hierarchy-based approach to respect
- Discourage any sort of discrimination within the organization
- Create and practice a strong set of organizational values
- Create awareness of respectful behaviors within organizations
- Have one-on-one discussions with employees about sensitive issues
- Avoid group conversations when giving constructive feedback
- Listen to employees and give importance to their input
- Be open-minded to absorb new ideas and listen to employees' views
- Always protect the dignity of employees
- Discourage office gossip and backbiting work cultures
- Encourage being respectful for end customers under any circumstances
- Encourage being respectful with business partners and vendors

5.2.1.4. Positive Communication

As a leader or manager, you need always to make sure you have positive communication, irrespective of the situation. Never include negativity, personal insults, or stereotypes in your conversation, even if you need to discuss an employee's failures. It is important that your tone and communication always remain positive.

You should start the conversation by recognizing the good work the employee or their team has done before you bring up their failures or mistakes. Even though it may be challenging at times to be optimistic if the employee becomes angry or defensive, strive to keep it as positive as you can.

When you bring up the shortcoming, don't make it seem as if you are blaming them. Simply discuss how they think they can improve. You want to help them become motivated to do better, not to feel bad for having failed. Give them the moral support to move on and achieve their goals successfully next time.

Positive communication does wonders for an employee's psychological health and has a vast potential to drive them to greater heights. If employees always get the feeling that the management is unhappy about every mistake, they will become demotivated and lack the drive to fix problems.

As a good leader, you need to clear this misconception by highlighting how much you value their contribution. Show them that a single mistake will not override all the good they have been doing for so long. This is an influential psychological factor that can drive employees to do even better because they feel the organization is willing to give them a chance to correct their mistake or shortcoming. With this style of communication and problem-handling, employees are automatically motivated to make sure they do not let down you or the organization again.

5. Team

5.2.1.4.1. How to Improve on Positive Communication

- Be optimistic in communications
- Don't let a bad mood take control of your communication
- Speak to employees from the heart
- Encourage positive communication from the top down and the bottom up
- Be helpful to employees in communications and outcomes
- Support your employees' morale
- Make the communications motivating, not demotivating
- Try to give good feedback wherever possible
- Obtain feedback from employees on improvements required
- Create a positive environment for employees to be heard
- Have conversations in a friendly and encouraging manner
- Avoid putting people down even in challenging situations
- Avoid creating any emotional damage
- Practice active listening in conversations
- Avoid discouraging ideas brought up by employees
- Always be logical when proving things incorrect
- Highlight the positive side of things prior to bringing up negatives
- Suggest improvements rather than bringing up shortcomings

5.2.1.5. Positive Competition

Competition, if done in a good way, can be beneficial for everyone. Positive competition usually occurs between employees, teams, and even organizations, mainly if they are spread across multiple territories or geographies. However, it needs to be closely monitored to ensure it does not get out of hand and become mean-spirited.

For example, if two teams are performing the same task, each team trying to do it better than the other can be taken as a simple example of positive competition. This should be encouraged because positive competition can deliver excellent outcomes. But there is sometimes a fine line between positive and hostile competition.

If employees try to compete with each other in a non-ethical way, it can lead to disaster. Therefore, the most important role a leader or manager needs to play is to ensure that the competition is positive and not negative and take measures to make the employees stick to ethical boundaries.

One other important factor to focus on is coming up with a rewarding structure built around values and ethics such as respect, integrity, and trust. When the rewards are centered around these things, employees tend to complete in a friendlier way.

There are no losers in positive competition. Some may have outperformed others, but in the end, everyone is a winner. And in the end, everyone should be rewarded. This is crucial to coming together next time with more courage and energy for a better and improved competition.

As a leader or manager, your role is to mediate and manage things smoothly and to ensure that guidelines and ethics are valued and adhered. In a nutshell, a positive completion as a whole is an accelerator for organizational growth. But it takes only a slight slip in focus to turn a positive competition into a negative one. Negative competition can drastically harm organizations. Therefore, it needs to be managed very carefully to derive the full benefit.

5.2.1.5.1. How to Improve on Positive Competition

Create awareness on what is meant by positive competition	Explain the purpose of positive competition	Have clear guidelines on ethics for positive competition
Make the environment a fun and encouraging one	Encourage employees to work with good faith	Explain the benefits a positive competition could bring to the table
Share valuable lessons and learnings	Drive positive competition for innovation and creativity	Avoid a culture of blame within the organization
Shuffle teams to give everyone a chance to work with others	Try to practice the positives identified across all teams	Focus on lessons learned at the end of each engagement
Encourage all teams and team members to practice positive competition	Encourage values like integrity and trust among teams	Encourage respect among fellow employees
Avoid the winners' and losers' mindsets within employees	Obtain feedback from employees and incorporate the important ones	Bring positive competition part of organizational culture

5.2.1.6. Incentives

Incentivizing employees is a proven way to keep motivation high. There are a few aspects that organizations need to keep in mind when it comes to incentive schemes. They need to be both strategically and practically managed. It must be something that an organization can run for a considerable period of time. Therefore, it is always recommended to structure such programs to increase gradually and incrementally. If it is stopped halfway due to financial or other challenges, it creates an immediate demotivation in the employees' minds. Therefore, it is best to avoid sudden changes to the program.

Incentives should never impact employees negatively. To be successful, they need to be practical and attainable. If it is not, it will demotivate employees and decrease their satisfaction and loyalty. Furthermore, it has to be attractive enough to drive someone toward achieving it.

When employees achieve unexpected and impressive things, especially during challenging times, these exceptional cases need to be given special rewards. Usually, this kind of achievement is not limited to a single person's contribution, even though it may seem like it. Therefore, it is essential to reward all who contributed to it.

While incentives do motivate people, inaccurate incentivization is often a demotivating factor. Therefore, you need to be very careful to ensure the whole process is done correctly so as not to defeat the purpose. You should also be very careful not to introduce bias and favoritism into your incentive plan. It must be driven purely by the positive nature of competition and performance.

There will still be failures and problems, despite your best efforts. Be sure to encourage these teams and individuals to keep up their morale and motivation so they can do better next time. If not, they will be disheartened, and their motivation level may drop drastically, making it nearly impossible for them to continue doing their jobs effectively. Such cases are usually almost at the winning point, and they just need a little encouragement to achieve it.

5. Team

5.2.1.6.1. How to Improve on Incentives

- Have the right budget allocation for incentives
- Make incentives attractive
- Link incentives to organizational goals and targets
- Make goals and targets achievable so the incentives are achievable too
- Make incentives timely and relevant
- Create awareness on employees on their incentive potentials
- Enable incentives based on achievement incrementally
- Ensure the incentive schemes are sustainable
- Enable incentives for special achievements
- Tie work quality to incentives as a core KPI
- Give employees adequate time to prove themselves
- Make the incentive process clear and structured
- Explain the calculations to employees to help them understand it
- Avoid favoritism or bias within the incentive process
- Remove any ambiguity of any KPIs linked to incentives
- Change incentive models based on new goals and targets
- Review lessons learned when the process is finished
- Make upskilling a key KPI for incentives

5.2.1.7. Team Outcomes

One of the key performance indicators is the overall team outcomes. However, this is also one of the most challenging areas to monitor for many reasons. There are many standard challenges when it comes to team outcomes.

One critical aspect is the differences among the individuals that make up a team. Each person will have a unique personality and skillset compared to the others. When teams are being given common goals, measuring their success becomes quite complex at times.

Two common reasons are that each can easily blame the others for the mistakes that led to the overall team's failure. On the other hand, there can be many individuals in a team who are willing to stretch themselves a bit more to cover up the shortcomings of their colleagues to ensure the team is driven to success.

As a leader or manager, your foremost duty must be transparency and visibility for any project that gets measured on a team's output. The most crucial part of a team's success is the positive attitude of the team members. They need to respect and help each other. Unless the values and attitude issues are addressed, the team can easily have recurring issues that may result in failure in many areas.

Furthermore, when a team is formed, it is essential to invest in team-building activities and allow the team to mingle outside of the context of work. The more the team understands each other, the easier it becomes for them to work together.

On the other hand, as a leader or manager, you should avoid pointing out individual shortcomings and not encourage a culture of people complaining about each other and their issues. Conversations always need to be team-centric, and praise and recognition need to be team-centric too. While you don't want to entertain gossip and complaining within the employees, you need to keep a significantly closer look on each individual's performance and potential issues, and you have to proactively ensure that problems are addressed before other employees bring it up as a complaint.

Furthermore, it is good to have sub-teams if the teams are too large to handle to ensure a smooth operation. This will help reduce the micro-management aspects when it comes to managing multiple teams.

5.2.1.7.1. How to Improve on Team Outcomes

- Create strong teams with balanced skill sets
- Conduct team-building exercises to improve bonding
- Encourage unity between teams
- Measure team outcomes and not individual performance
- Consider user personalities when teams are formed
- Make team evaluations transparent
- Create the "one team" mindset among members
- Encourage teams to take part in sports activities as a team
- Provide team goals and targets
- Work closely with teams to address team issues
- Give teams adequate time to settle prior to giving core task assignments
- Recognize exceptional team players
- Have reward schemes in place for recognitions
- Keep continuous communication with employees
- Ensure the right team leads are placed within teams
- Have right dispute resolution policies in place
- Shuffle teams over a period for better engagement
- Apply the lessons learnt to further improve on the team building process

5.2.1.8. Flexibility

Flexibility is one of the key drivers of motivation. However, this aspect works both ways—from an organization toward the employee and from an employee toward the organization.

There are some standard aspects organizations could offer flexibility on, and some others need to be dealt with on a case-by-case basis. Some general aspects of flexibility could be offering flexible working hours, flexible attire, flexible options for remote work, and many others. However, such flexibilities may vary based on the nature of the business and the type of operations.

While some jobs require an onsite presence, others may not. Let's take the example of someone who is a delivery vehicle driver. In this case, remote work is not an option as the job by nature requires the person to be present. On the other hand, some other jobs require a fixed working time. Therefore, there is not a single strategy that all organizations could adopt to be flexible. It varies drastically, based on the nature of business.

In an overall sense, flexibility refers to be having a flexible nature of understanding among the employee and the organization, where each of them could go an extra mile to support the other when it comes to things that are different than the normal cause of actions. Respect and empathy have a more significant role to play to have flexibility. Each should respect and prioritize the other in achieving the overall objective. Organizations need to have a positive outlook toward adjusting themselves to the best level possible to accommodate an employee's priorities and vice versa.

One crucial aspect to avoid is the misuse of flexibility. This could lead to devastating situations both ways. As a leader or manager, you need to ensure that none of the employees are abusing the organization's flexibility. On the other hand, you need to ensure the organization is also never moving into decisions that could abuse employee flexibility. Once either party abuses the flexibility, it will be very challenging to bring things back to normal. Furthermore, one person's action could negatively impact all other fellow employees, and one wrong case of abusing an employee's flexibility could lead to the dissatisfaction of the rest of the employees.

Therefore, flexibility needs to be provided and managed care for the desired outcomes to be achieved.

5. Team

5.2.1.8.1. How to Improve on Flexibility

- Have a flexible working time policy for permitted roles
- Have flexible work locations for permitted roles
- Explain the relationship of trust vs flexibility
- Create a work culture to be flexible wherever it is possible
- Educate employees on the flexibility policies
- Ensure terms on flexibility and constantly updated
- Educate employees on consequences of flexibility misuse
- Avoid loopholes for potential flexibility misuses
- Speak to employees on organizational values
- Leadership should have an open mindset toward flexible work
- Cross-train people for reduced dependency
- Create a team-driven culture
- Allow employees to shift work tracks if possible
- Keep close monitoring on flexible arrangements to avoid any gaps
- Leadership puts flexibility in practice
- Learn from mistakes and keep them from recurring
- Take right actions on any potential abuse of flexibility
- Incorporate employee feedback to improve flexibility aspects

5.2.1.9. Continuous Recognition and Rewarding

Recognition and reward are fundamental drivers of motivation in employees. However, these need to be consistent and continuous. One-time recognition and rewarding could create a sudden increase in motivation; however, it will not last long.

Sudden peaks and drops of motivation levels could have long-term impacts within organizations as they result in unpredictable results. Whether it be positive or negative, organizations usually prefer to have predictable outcomes.

Let us take this example of a sudden motivation within an organization that has resulted from more outcomes within a given period. However, as was unpredicted, the organization may not be prepared to make the most of the sudden benefit. On the other hand, it raises the bar for expectations, and when this is not continued, it may result in disappointment. Therefore, recognition and rewarding have to be strategically managed.

Recognition and rewards may not only be limited to finances. There are different forms of reward. Some are honorary, and some are financial. The goodwill and the trust an organization places on an employee is also a form of recognition.

As a leader or manager, you must be responsible for developing a strategic and sustainable rewarding and recognition model or a methodology that can be applied based on performance.

Favoritism and bias need to be kept out of the process as they could easily lead to demotivated and disgruntled employees. An organization needs to have a clear set of guidelines on how the recognition policies work. There have to be clear criteria that are easily quantifiable and measurable. The process needs to be transparent, and you should have a clear understanding and justification for any choices made. Consistency and continuity are the two most important qualities to keep in mind.

The evaluation criteria have to be put forward in a manner that each employee has a fair chance to achieve it. While some may be work-related, others could be on other aspects such as special talents. (i.e., such as singing in an official awards ceremony or a talent show).Overall, each employee should be given a chance to prove themselves and their abilities

5. Team

on various aspects, and the organization's rewards and recognition model should accommodate it.

5.2.1.9.1. How to Improve Continuous Recognition and Rewarding

- Plan recognition and rewarding with sustainability in mind
- Maintain sustainable budget allocations for rewards and recognition
- Revisit budgets to make sure rewards are relevant
- Obtain employee feedback on the rewards and recognition
- Ensure rewards and recognitions are motivating
- Tie rewards and recognitions to organizational goals and targets
- Educate employees on rewards and recognitions
- Ensure that rewards and recognitions are continued over years
- Make rewards and recognition a critical organizational priority
- Make the rewards achievable in a practical sense
- Put programs in place to help employees gain rewards and recognition
- Coach employees to be successful within the organization
- Ensure recognitions are given to the right people for the right reasons
- Make sure the recognitions are emotionally motivating
- Avoid any favoritism or bias in performance evaluations
- Avoid any discrimination on the rewards and recognition process
- Keep the rewards and recognition process transparent
- Try to improve the rewards and recognition on a continuous basis

5.2.2. Loyalty

5.2.2.1. Investing in Employees

Employees are the most valued asset of any organization. Investing in employees is one key driver of loyalty. Employees like to be in organizations that take care of them and allow them to advance their careers. Investing in employees is a win-win for both the organization and the employee.

Organizations invest in employees to train them on skills that the organization could benefit from. On the other hand, employees are upskilling themselves, which will never go waste as it could advance their careers.

Having loyal employees is one of the biggest wins an organization can get. Loyalty is not gained overnight. It is a process of the employee feeling valued and treated well and being taken care of in the right manner. Loyal employees bring endless benefits to an organization. They advocate for your organizations and spread your name throughout the community. They always work toward the best interest of the organization. They do their best to help the organizations to succeed.

Investing in employees could vary from a range of different methods. While some of them could involve a direct cost, some may not cost much in terms of money.

Giving an employee a most straightforward career path and opportunities to grow is also a way to invest in their success. The more opportunities they gain, the more chances they have to grow.

As a leader or manager, you need to ensure that you maintain employee loyalty. One incident could result in an employee losing the loyalty they have toward an organization. Once lost, it can cost significant effort, time, and investment to gain it back, and even then, it will never be the same as before it was lost.

Organizations need to have strategies, policies, and initiatives to improve employee loyalty. This needs to be one core aspect of the organizational goals.

5. Team

5.2.2.1.1. How to Improve on Investing in Employees

- Have the right budget allocation for employee investments
- Establish a solid qualification criterion
- Find the right talents to be invested
- Carry out the investments on an outcome basis
- Educate employees on their opportunities
- Allocate an annual quota for such investments
- Put together a model for the organization to be benefitted by the investments
- Create a growth path for employees within the organization
- Create promotions and hikes based on performance and growth paths
- Put focus on employee well-being and mental health
- Invest in employees for upskilling
- Invest in employees to gain international exposure
- Always focus on internal promotions for suitable positions
- Leadership should continuously upskill themselves
- Evaluate the skill levels to identify the gaps within organization
- Hire subject matter experts to build right skills within organization
- Focus on improving employee loyalty
- Put right measures in place to evaluate employee loyalty

5.2.2.2. Open-Door Policy

As we discussed in one of the previous sections, an open-door policy can benefit an organization. It can contribute toward increasing employee loyalty and cut down the hierarchy and the roadblocks on communications. It also creates an accessible environment for the employees to express themselves.

Employee loyalty is strongly impacted by how much the employees perceive that an organization values them. Having fewer roadblocks in reaching the top empowers employees to feel heard and understood. It allows for more personal conversations and reduces fear and intimidation about speaking to management.

On the other hand, it helps the leadership get a better sense of the things happening on the ground level of the organization. This knowledge is very beneficial in helping the leaders make the right choices for the company. Without an open-door culture, it is much harder for the managers to understand the viewpoint of their employees. These insights may give a different point of view and a perspective for the leaders, allowing them to think in alignment with the employee thought process.

The openness of the leadership is a powerful psychological factor that helps drive employees to do their best for the company. They are more likely to take risks and extend themselves for the betterment of the organization, even if it does not directly benefit them.

We highly recommend that leaders and managers practice an open-door policy. It is an indirect, less costly investment an organization can make to achieve a very loyal workforce who will always go the extra mile for the betterment of the organization.

5. Team

5.2.2.2.1. How to Improve on an Open-Door Policy

- Leadership should be open for employee discussions
- Remove the hierarchy restrictions on employee communications
- Try to have informal chats with employees and peers
- Try to keep conversations within lunches or coffee breaks, etc.
- Help employees to be confident about speaking to leadership
- Show a positive attitude toward employees when they share their concerns
- Be an active listener so you can understand employee problems
- Help employees when they are mentally down
- Respect employee emotions and feelings
- Understand the employee gaps when having conversations
- Be a mentor
- Show you're a good leader by your actions
- Be patient in employee conversations
- Obtain employee feedback on areas to improve
- Be kind and nice to employees
- Always welcome employees for a chat when they need it
- Allocate some time in your calendar to talk to employees
- Apply lessons learned to improve the open-door process

5.2.2.3. Training and Development

Training and development is a continuous improvement activity that organizations need to focus on. This has to be an organization-wide initiative.

Upskilling employees is a journey without an end. There is not a defined deadline that makes any organization fully trained. Every day, employees learn new things, technologies evolve, and markets change. Therefore, it is essential that organizations keep in pace with the rapid nature of the market and adapt to it.

Training and development is an investment that an organization needs to make in increasing the value of its human capital.

On the other hand, it needs to be well received and positively accepted by the employees. Primarily, organizations need to create awareness among employees about the benefits it could bring them and the risks if they do not upskill themselves. Unless this message is clear, training and development will only be something that is pushed by the organization, and employees will only do what they have to to get through it.

Once the objectives are clear, it gives clarity to employees as to why training is essential. When they realize this, they will understand the value of the offered training. Then they will realize that the company considers them worthwhile.

Furthermore, employees should be given opportunities once they have proven themselves in the areas they are already trained in.

Retraining is another important area organizations need to focus as the grasping capacity may vary from one employee to another. There has to be a clear evaluation mechanism for organizations to evaluate the effectiveness of training, and employees should be given an opportunity to showcase how much training has helped them do things faster and more efficiently. The overall value realization needs to be closely monitored for effective outcomes.

5. Team

5.2.2.3.1. How to Improve on Training & Development

Analyze the organization, employees, and skills required	Identify the skill gaps present within the organization	Put together an organizational training requirement plan
Obtain the required budgets for the T&D requirements	Identify potential candidates to be invested in	Obtain feedback from employees to understand their training requirements
Create a train the trainer model within the organization	Continuously evaluate the effectiveness of training	Revisit training plans and update them based on current trends and needs
Put in place a model to recover the organizational investment of T&D	Assess how trainings could impact overall loyalty	Speak to employees to hear their ideas
Understand how employees feel they have benefited from T&D efforts	Conduct employee surveys to see the impact of such initiatives	Tell employees how the organization is focused on helping them improve
Ensure all employees are upskilled	Help employees understand how upskilling has increased their value	Apply lessons learned for future improvements

5.2.2.4. Perks and Benefits

Employee perks and benefits are indeed another avenue that an organization can use to improve employee loyalty. Perks and benefits vary organization to another and also among employee groups.

One of the most critical aspects any organization should consider on this is to make sure they come up with a sustainable model. If not, this could be a demotivating factor for employees. There have been many instances where organizations have started such initiatives without proper evaluation and have shown substantial negative impacts. Such perks or benefits may be dependable based on various aspects of an organization such as individual employee performance, overall organizational performance, team performance, and many other factors.

Furthermore, some organizations have a culture of adopting a bonus for various festivals, based on the organizational strategy and cultures. While these could individually motivate employees, organizations need to make sure such would not go against their objectives.

When such perks are considered, organizations need to develop a very transparent and evaluation-based model that decides how much of a perk each is entitled to from a logical basis. If the model is unclear, employees will start questioning each other and comparing their perks compared to their colleagues', especially those at parallel levels.

Therefore, the ambiguity elements of perks need to be avoided, and there has to be a fair justification on how and why a person is entitled to a perk with entitlement limits. It is essential to educate the employees on such areas and keep clear communication to employees. Furthermore, it is recommended that organizations put forward a policy to keep such information confidential.

Similar to keeping the salary information confidential, organizations need to come up with polices to keep perks and benefits among employees confidential. This discourages an employee from talking about their benefits entitlement with another employee in an official conversation. Such policies would keep internal communication low and reduce any disputes or misunderstandings spread across a different groups of employees.

5. Team

As a leader or manager, you need to ensure that your organization has a clear policy on perks and benefits and there is continuous awareness made to your employees to ensure they are up to date on it at any given point in time.

5.2.2.4.1. How to Improve on Perks and Benefits

- Assess the current perks and benefits in detail
- Identify the gaps in the current perks and benefits
- Identity how to improve perks and benefits in a sustainable manner
- Tie perks and benefits to performance and outcome
- Emphasize a performance-driven incentives model
- Review the company's position compared to competition
- Allocate required budgets for maintaining the perks and benefits
- Focus on employee well-being elements in perks and benefits
- Obtain employee feedback to understand their views
- Ensure the perks and benefits plans are not dropped halfway
- Highlight to employees the value of available schemes
- Assess how such schemes improve employee loyalty
- Conduct pre- and post-assessments to understand specific impact of schemes
- Ensure perks and benefits are impactful
- Keep the evaluation criteria transparent

Assess employee mental well-being and happiness	Assess the staff turnover rates to determine the impact of such schemes	Use the lessons learned for future improvements in these areas

5.2.2.5. Extended Focus

Extended focus is an exciting area that has proven to give the best results regarding loyalty. It expands the focus one step away from the employees to be concerned with their families too.

This is indeed a very successful approach to effectively improve employee loyalty. When employees feel that their organization is concern about them and the well-being of their families, they will automatically align toward loyalty.

An employee's family has a significant contribution to their decisions. When the entire family has a positive outlook toward the company, the employee will automatically focus on it as well. Some activities that could further this are family outings sponsored by the company that allow families to mingle and get to know each other. The organization might also hold a ceremony to recognize the children of employees who have excelled in their school programs or sports.

In simple terms, it means extending the focus to celebrate the success of the employees' family members. This creates an inclusion within the families, and even the employees' children will automatically start building a positive outlook toward the workplace of their parents.

Organizations can also extend their support in helping employees' families by taking part in their sorrows. This can be implemented by having a welfare fund to support employee families burdened with a sudden calamity such as a natural disaster or the loss of a loved one. This could include financially aiding such employees.

These kinds of programs spread quickly by word of mouth and help to build a positive image of the company in the community.

As a leader or manager, you should ensure that you have a suitable mechanism in place to find out about employee issues and have policies

5. Team

to extend support for them. It is critical to make these initiatives sustainable and also to create awareness among employees to understand their entitlements too.

5.2.2.5.1. How to Improve on Extended Focus

Have focus on employees' extended circle	Be concerned about employees' families and well-being	Create organizational welfare funds to support employee families
Be empathetic toward employee family members and their challenges	Give prominence to employee emotional needs	Allow employee families to bond together
Create schemes to improve employees' children's education and well-being	Give recognition to employees' children's special achievements	Sponsor employees' children when they meet criteria
Create a positive impression about organization within employee families	Make leadership sensitive to employees and their family needs	Assess how these programs increase employee loyalty
Carry out surveys to read the mind of employees	Put to action meaningful feedback received	Have policies in organization in place to have extended focus

Keep conversation not only limited to work, but also about family & well-being	Be supportive for employees during critical junctures in life	Apply lessons learned for future improvements in these areas

5.2.3. Life Balance

5.2.3.1. Awareness of Work-Life Balance

Work-life balance is one of the most critical areas to focus on for a happy workforce. As leaders or managers, you need to be aware that only a workforce with the right work-life balance has a better chance of sustainability. There have to be organizational policies with clear guidelines on the expected work hours of an employee.

While there can be occasional exceptions, organizations should not expect employees to work so much they are unable to pay attention to their lives. Maintaining a work-life balance is partly the organization's responsibility, but there are some aspects that are purely dependent on the employee, and these have to be improved from an employee standpoint.

The first aspect of the company's responsibility is to create awareness among employees on how to balancing work and life. Furthermore, organizational policies, goals, and strategies have to be developed keeping in mind the aspects of the work-life balance.

Awareness can be created by sending communications and creating awareness campaigns within the organization to help employees understand how a balance can be achieved. Furthermore, managers need to be educated on the processes they need to adhere to when assigning work. While some organizations have policies, some managers or leaders do not adhere to them. In such instances, employees could make complaints to outside authorities.

Therefore, as a leader or manager, you need to be firm in practicing work-life balance and should be an agent of change and advocate of it, setting a good example by your actions. This will encourage employees to live a balanced life, which will eventually be a win for both the organization and the employee.

5. Team

5.2.3.1.1. How to Improve Awareness of Work-Life Balance

Create awareness on work-life balance	Create mandatory leave plans for employees to balance work and life	Be sensitive not to invade personal time of employees
Teach employees to be efficient during work hours	Educate employees to start work on time and finish on time	Educate employees that dedication does not mean working extra hours
Assess employees on efficiency and effectiveness	Evaluate employee workloads to see if there are any overloads	Ensure organization policies address work-life balance
Allow flexible work time wherever it permits	Allow flexible workplace arrangement for roles when possible	Assess employees on their outcomes
Provide paid time off for employees to spend time with their families	Educate employees on mental well-being	Be cooperative to help employees achieve work-life balance
Lead by example of work-life balance	Emphasize employees that rest is needed for quality output in work	Obtain feedback to improve on these areas and incorporate valid feedback

5.2.3.2. Effective Usage of Time

Time is a valuable resource. Practical usage of time has a direct impact on having a work-life balance. This could be an effective use of office time for work and personal time. While employees are required to work on an 8-5 job mostly five days a week, some organizations could offer part-time work. However, most require a minimum number of work hours to compensate their employees.

The key to achieving work-life balance is ensuring employees are giving a hundred percent focus during work hours. Unless employees are fully focused, they will become less likely to achieve the expected outcome, and then they will need to put in extra hours of work to complete their work. This could have indirect cost impacts on organizations due to excessive resources consumption. With the remote work conditions that have reduced to some level, this can harm the other employees too.

Simply because many tasks within an organization are interlinked, if one person fails to complete their job on time, all the others who are directly or indirectly dependent on it could also be working extra time and putting extra effort to complete and cover up a delay of one person. Therefore, ineffective usage of time can have substantial impacts on an overall organization. And when the employee misses their family time, that could lead to other personal challenges, and they will soon start to lose focus on the job. A sound mind is essential for a good outcome. Ineffective usage of time can lead to a non-sound mind, and employees may eventually be rushing things off to meet deadlines.

As a leader or manager, you need to ensure that you take the necessary steps to ensure that work-life balance is maintained at work by the practical usage of time by the employees. If this is not achieved due to an issue from the employee or due to an indirect impact from another employee, it needs to be addressed immediately for the benefit of the overall organization without any delays.

5. Team

5.2.3.2.1. How to Improve on Effective Usage of Time

Assess employee inefficiencies	Identify the root causes for the employee inefficiencies	Plan on how to fix employee inefficiencies
Obtain employee feedback for their inefficiencies	Address any challenges causing the employee inefficiencies	Set standard timings for each process in place
Assess and understand the causes for any exceptions	Educate employees on how to be efficient	Remove any potential employee distractions within workplace
Tie efficiency KPIs to employees' overall evaluations	Tie incentives and perks to efficiencies	Identify the savings made by improving employee efficiency
Help employees to stay focused	Ensure team targets are set for overall efficiency	Avoid chances for taking shortcuts to achieve efficiency
Recognize efficient workers and reward them	Leadership should provide examples of efficiency	Apply lessons learned for future improvements

5.2.3.3. Cross-Training

Cross-training of resources can help organizations achieve work-life balance in a more indirect perspective. By effective cross-training of resources, organizations can effectively cut down the amount they depend on each employee. In the event of an emergency, organizations will always have the ability to seek the support of another employee to cover a given task.

Furthermore, sudden market conditions may require an organization to stretch more than they usually do. In such cases, when multiple resources are available, organizations can efficiently distribute the work to multiple employees without overburdening one person.

The more independent an organization is from an individual, the more it will become a win for both the given individual and the organization.

As leaders or managers, you need to consider cross-training as a wide organizational initiative to ensure it is done effectively for all possible roles. Some roles, however, can present challenges to cross-training resources due to their nature, complexity, and skill scarcity. In such cases, it is recommended that organizations have employees shadow critical roles to get at least of how the job is done.

This will be more helpful than not knowing anything. At least this way, in the event of an emergency, another person will be able to carry out the job with some supervision from the person responsible for it.

Organizations also need to have a mechanism to recognize resources that are good at multiple streams or areas as they can be critical to an organization for sustainability. Organizations need to take necessary actions and strategies to ensure that these resources are not overburdened. Sometimes, this may automatically happen because they are good at various things: All such tasks may lead to them.

There has to be a proper control done and supervision to ensure all of the resources are not overburdened. It can sometimes happen that specialized resources are overburdened for the simple reason that they are very successful at any tasks that are assigned to them. This puts them in an unfair situation where they are tasked more and more as they continue to deliver good outcomes.

5.2.3.3.1. How to Improve on Cross Training

- Identify the potential for cross-training
- Identify the right candidates for cross-training
- Emphasize the importance of learning a new skill
- Provide employees with opportunities to cross-train if they are willing
- Assess the short-term issues during the learning curve
- Put measures in place to minimize the impacts during the learning curve
- Recognize the employees based on their ability to learn new skills
- Give rewards based on trainability and skills of employees
- Leaders should provide examples of ability to learn new skills
- Strategically reduce employee dependability
- Understand employees' views on any shortcomings and challenges
- Incorporate valid feedback for future improvements
- Create cross-training as a team objective
- Assess team outcomes based on cross-training
- Allow employees to shadow when they need more training
- Motivate employees on their cross-training efforts
- Make cross-training part of organizational culture
- Use lessons learned for future improvements

5.2.3.4. Paid Time Off

Paid time off is essential in bringing a good work-life balance to employees. Sometimes, employees may be reluctant to take time off even though they are stressed out due to their excessive work. Employers should encourage employees to take time if they are stressed out.

There are different types of schemes organizations could effectively adopt in coming up with adequate paid time off for the most deserving employees. Some time could be structured in a way that is earned due to some continuous work conditions. For example, a company that generally has an 8-hour shift is expecting an employee to work 9-hour shifts for five days continuously, making them eligible for a paid day off to compensate them for their efforts and hard work. By doing this, employees are recognized for the extra mile they go or the extra efforts they put in.

Organizations can also give leave to help people with important moments in their lives such as anniversaries, paternal leave, etc. By doing this, organizations are giving employees more chances to give themselves a break. This is very important for employees because a good rest helps employees improve their effectiveness. Too much work and stress can cut down employee creativity and motivation, resulting in less outcomes. Looking forward to time off will also help motivate them to do their best.

While there can be many statutory guidelines organizations need to keep complaints to a minimum, it is recommended to do more than the basic compliances to create a positive attitude with employees. As leaders and managers, you also need to make sure employees are aware of and take advantage of the leave they are entitled to. It is beneficial for them and the company. Time off needs to be encouraged by management, and there have to be some KPIs to measure a good work-life balance to ensure employees to see this as something positive.

5. Team

5.2.3.4.1. How to Improve on Paid Time Off

Create paid time-off organizational policies	Make paid time off mandatory	Assess employee outcomes pre & post time off
Allow employees more time to spend with their families	Educate employees on why leave is important to reset themselves	Be supportive to employees on their vacation plans
Have employees cross-trained to reduce dependence	Respect employee time off and avoid calling or texting during vacations	Always have backup staff present when someone is on leave
Ensure proper handover happens prior to taking leave	Educate employees on work and life priorities	Try to encourage vacation leave during off-peak periods
Obtain employee feedback on any improvements needed	Encourage full team leave after critical projects are completed	Plan team bonding outings on time off if possible
Avoid carrying forward time off unless for a good reason	Be accommodating of employee requests for leave	Use lessons learned to improve on this area

5.2.3.5. Corporate Initiatives

There are many corporate initiatives organizations can encourage for employee betterment and work-life balance. Such initiatives need to be organization-wide and have to be driven on a top-down approach.

Employee wellness is another area organizations need to put more focus on. Employee wellness refers to both physical wellness and psychological wellness too. It is essential to have a healthy workforce as this can support an organization in many aspects. A workforce that is fit and healthy both physically and psychologically is proven to produce good results. Healthy individuals generally are not lazy. Furthermore, when they are psychologically sound, they can put their entire focus on the work they do.

While employees can have different levels of focus, there is not much an organization can do for a person if he is not focused. An employee with average focus can complete a task per expectations. However, someone who is super-focused is capable of producing exceptional results.

While organizations could take actions against employees who are not focused, there is not much an organization do: If people are not super-focused, that is above the minimum expectation. On the other hand, when employees put in more than their best, it quickly results in organizations achieving success with outcomes that are generally proven to be exceptional.

It is essential that organizations take this lead because employees tend not to give importance to these aspects as they are busy with their work. They may even consider themselves too busy to do daily routines to improve their health.

When it's run at a company level, especially if the leadership is taking part, employees will automatically be motivated to participate. You need to ensure that you take all required steps and investments to run such initiatives at a company level for your organization to be concerned with the well-being of their employees both physically and psychologically.

5. Team

5.2.3.5.1. How to Improve on Corporate Initiatives

- Focus on employee well-being initiatives
- Allocate adequate budgets for the required corporative initiatives
- Educate employees on the importance of taking part
- Identify the employees' priority to participate
- Focus on initiatives with employee health
- Create a work environment for employees to be healthy
- Plan for initiatives that are sustainable
- Assess the benefits for employees
- Obtain employee feedback to obtain their views
- Assess how such initiatives improve employee loyalty to the organization
- Assess how such initiatives improve employee retention
- Assess how such initiatives improve the public image of the organization
- Assess how such initiatives help employees improve their focus
- Conduct continuous feedback to assess the success of any initiative
- Make these initiatives mandatory across all levels
- Leadership should be actively engaged in such initiatives
- Any failed initiatives should be replaced with better ones
- Use lessons learned for any future improvements

5.2.3.6. Outcome-Based KPIs

Traditionally, organizations had KPIs set for employee time, attendance, punctuality, and many other aspects that did not have much effect on outcomes. Coming to work on time was always a critical KPI for assessment. However, in recent times, things have changed to a level where organizations are now much more focused on the output of an employee, irrespective of how punctual they are or if they come to work every day.

Generally speaking, KPIs need to be always outcome-based. This is simply because what matters most to an organization is the outcome a person achieves. Whether or not they achieve it by being punctual or if they even come to work or not does not really matter much.

As a leader or manager, our recommendation is to ensure your KPIs are always measured by the outcome and not any other aspects that are not relevant to an output. When KPIs are set this manner, employees will have a lot of flexibility when it comes to achieving their set targets, and it can also give them a good work-life balance. The flexibility of the workplace has a lot to do with the work-life balance of the employee.

As a leader or manager, you should make a substantial contribution to understanding which of the employee goals are meaningful and have a direct link to the output. Remote working is one such area that can provide flexibility to the employee if they have some personal commitments that require them to be at home like childcare or parental care.

On the other hand, some jobs require a person to perform a specific task at a given location. For example, if we take a job of front-line customer care executive, they may have to be present physically to greet customers. In this case, there is only a little an organization can do in achieving flexibility.

Organizations need to spend some quality time reviewing their KPIs and goals to understand which aspects of a KPI or a measurement align with the outcome and which do not. If something does not directly impact the output but is keeping things inflexible for an employee, you need to take that aspects off the KPIs.

While each organization has different business models and ways of doing things, each may approach this problem differently than the others.

5. Team

The key takeaway from this section is to always ensure that the KPIs are relevant and not unnecessarily inflexible. Always focus on the outcome and allow the employees to work in a way they are comfortable with and that allows them to achieve their outcomes.

5.2.3.6.1. How to Improve Outcome-Based KPIs

Assess existing organizational KPIs	Identify how far they are outcome driven	Assess the outcomes vs KPIs to make improvements
Ensure the KPIs are unambiguous	Educate employees about the KPIs and outcomes	Obtain employee feedback on any improvements needed
Assess the practicality of the KPIs and tied outcomes	Educate employees on how they can achieve their outcomes	Support employees on their path to achieve KPIs successfully
Assess if the measurements criteria are precise and accurate	Gradually improve KPIs over a period of time	Change the outcomes based on market needs if required
Have incentives and recognition in place to motive employees	Identify the potential failure points and provide corrective measures	Encourage employees in achieving their KPIs and outcomes

| Improve employee morale | Obtain external expertise to improve on KPIs and outcomes | Use lessons learned for any future improvements |

5.2.3.7. Flexibility

As explained in the above section, flexibility is an aspect each organization needs to focus on to achieve their desired outcomes. Each job will have a different level of flexibility in achieving the set objectives. However, flexibility is an element that is tightly integrated with trust. Trust is generally a two-way street. It has to go from employers to employees and vice versa.

Trust is the key for an organization in developing a flexible work culture. The flexibility of work can vary in multiple aspects and areas. It can include workplaces, work times, quality of deliverables, availability, and many other aspects.

For example, working times could be made flexible if the job does not require a person to start and finish at a given time. Furthermore, workplaces could be flexible if a job does not require a person to be at the office for a specific task. Then again, this depends on the type of work.

On the other hand, deliverable quality is also something that an organization could be flexible with, where for each task, if there is a set quality that needs to be met at a minimum, anything above that quality could be an acceptable delivery. This may vary from each product and service a company offers to the line of business.

Furthermore, the flexibility of availability could be identified as how important it is for a specific person to be present for a specific job. As we discussed before, with cross-training, the availability aspect of the employees could be made flexible. For an example, if a meeting requires the presence of some individual, and that individual cannot make it for some reason, then an organization can easily assign some other employee for this job, and this could offer some flexibility to all the employees.

The fundamental takeaway from this is that organizations need to make sure they put their primary focus on things that are important and worthwhile. If there is room for organizations to offer some flexibility to their employees, they should take steps and make efforts to offer it. On the other hand, organizations need to create the required awareness for the employees to clarify how trust and reliability are key drivers for organizations to consider flexible.

If both organizations and employees combine their best efforts to make it work, it will be a win-win situation for both parties.

5.2.4. Strengthening Self-Confidence

5.2.4.1. Coaching Employees

Coaching is a critical area in building employee self-confidence. Employees who are confident about their abilities and potential will achieve more significant outcomes. Employees who lack self-confidence believe they are not capable of doing a given task in the right manner. Furthermore, when employees do not have the required knowledge to work on a task, this will also tend to bring down their self-confidence levels. As a leader or manager, your duty is to coach each employee in the proper manner, building up their self-confidence.

Firstly, you need to make them believe that you trust them to do the assigned task. Your trust in them as a leader or manager is the first aspect that can help them boost their self-confidence.

Secondly, you may have to guide them on areas like problem-solving. As a leader or manager, you may have an excellent understanding of how to work out a methodical approach in finding a solution for a problem. It is your duty to coach your subordinates and the employees on how to look at a difficult problem and what approaches they should be taking to resolve it. You have to be a mentor and a coach to them, and you may have to support them in addressing their problems by working with them. Once they get used to a particular style of working, employees will automatically start applying this knowledge to other areas.

On-the-job coaching on the challenges faced on the job is one of the most effective ways to work together. It would be best if you always allowed the employee to take the lead and simply support them in their decision-making process. Once this is practiced for awhile, employees will then be ready to make decisions on their own. This is a journey of grooming backed by coaching and guidance that will achieve success over time.

5.2.4.1.1. How to Improve on Coaching Employees

Identify the employees who require the coaching	Identify the gaps that need to be coached on	Identify the coaching approach (internal/external)
List the objectives of coaching and the outcomes expected	Allocate adequate budget/time required for coaching	Educate the employees on their coaching approach
Assign the coaches to the employees to be coached	Obtain feedback from employees on their expectations	Address any valid gap that is identified
Conduct reviews to understand the progress of the coaching program	Address any gaps identified during the coaching program	Post completion, analyze how far the objectives are met
Obtain feedback from the coach on the challenges faced	Put the knowledge in to action to identify any further gap areas	Identify the employees who succeeded in coaching
Identify employees to coach junior employees	Keep the coaching process on a continuous basis	Make use of the lessons learned for future use

5.2.4.2. Embrace Ideas

Different employees have different thinking patterns and abilities. However, as a leader or manager, you need to make sure that you have a positive approach toward the ideas put forward by your employees. Embracing ideas and creating a positive environment for the employees to come up with better ideas will eventually support employees to come up with more great ideas.

There are many occasions where organizations have been proven to gain more tremendous success by hearing the ideas of their employees. There can be situations where employees could come up with ideas that are not worthwhile pursuing. In such cases, as a leader or manager, you need to take a patient and gentle approach in explaining why those ideas will not work. Unless you share your thoughts about it, employees may not have clarity. Once the reason and proper guidance is given on, employees will eventually fall into the right track of thinking. Once they get aligned to the proper track, they will slowly begin to develop ideas that could be worth exploring.

No idea, good or bad, should ever be rejected or discouraged out of hand. When employees feel humiliated or discouraged, they will lose interest in coming up with better ideas. This will stop them from volunteering any ideas. Furthermore, as a leader, you need to create an environment that is open for innovations and ideas by putting initiatives in place to assist the process.

On the other hand, embracing new ideas should not have any connection to the organizational hierarchy. Someone in a higher position should never show reluctance to consider a great idea put forward by someone in a lower position. These need to be the culture changes in an organization, and there has to be a framework put in place to evaluate ideas before they get lost in conversations. Any idea that gets rejected or pushed to a later stage should have valid reasoning as to why so that everyone will be clear on why that decision was made.

Finally, an excellent rewards program must be in place to encourage people whose ideas are taken into consideration and implemented. This will motivate others to come up with great ideas too.

Overall, the key takeaway from this section is that ideas should be always be welcomed and evaluated, and good ideas should be implemented without delay to keep innovation running within an organization. This is beneficial to the overall organizational growth.

5.2.4.2.1. How to Improve on Embracing Ideas

- Be open to new ideas
- Encourage employees to bring in new ideas
- Create a positive environment for employees to bring in new ideas
- Create an innovative drive culture within the organization
- Allow employees to spearhead some of the ideas they bring
- Reward employees for the better ideas brought up
- Ensure employees are not discouraged when bad ideas are brought up
- Run organizational initiatives to bring new ideas
- Create a workplace to help employees increase creativity
- Educate employees on the importance of innovation
- Encourage employees to think out of the box
- Try to fail fast when new ideas are implemented
- Do not discourage failure when new things are attempted
- Leadership should set an example by being creative and innovative
- Expose employees to new ways of thinking and problem-solving
- Make innovativeness as a key KPI within the organization
- Allocate adequate budgets for innovative idea execution
- Use the lessons learned for future improvements

5.2.4.3. Showing Respect

Respect is a valuable element that needs to exist within organizations. Showing respect has to be part of organizational culture. All humans want to be treated with respect.

As a manager, you must take the lead in putting this culture into practice. Showing respect could span many elements like communication, facial expression, body language, behavior, respecting emotions and priorities, and many others.

When it comes to communications, any employee in an organization has to be respectful toward their fellow employees. There has to be an organizational code of conduct that defines the boundaries of communication.

Verbal abuse should be strictly avoided, and the organizational policies should have protections and prosecutions for any verbal abuse toward an employee irrespective of the position of the abuser. Employees also need to be respectful in their facial expressions and body language. Some things to avoid should be sarcasm or sarcastic expressions, laughing and making inappropriate comments, disrespecting a person's view, etc.

Furthermore, organizations need to take strict measures in ensuring that employees' emotions are valued and respected. Each employee may be at different levels of emotional control. Some may break into tears at the smallest provocation. Leaders and managers need to set an example in handling sensitive situations with the utmost respect.

Last but not least, employee priorities need to be respected. Each employee has their own priorities in their life. Organizations need to take careful measures in making sure employee priorities are well-considered and respected. Some examples of this could be life events such as weddings or anniversaries, the accomplishments of their children, or even personal emergencies of their loved ones or close contacts. In such cases, employees may require time and effort to deal with these events.

When employees request time off or a flexible arrangement for such situations, organizations need to take due respect and consider these priorities as important as the employee does. While it may sound like not an urgent priority for you, it may have a major impact on an employee. Therefore, as a leader, you should avoid advising employees to deprioritize their priorities to focus on work-related elements. You might address it by delegating some tasks to others to allow the employee to focus on their priorities.

5.2.4.4. Failing Fast

Failing fast comes into the picture when organizations or employees try newer things.

Not all attempts made will always bring success. There are many times such attempts end up being a failure. Failing fast is especially important because the time and effort used on something is less when things fail fast. Whenever a new thing is tried, it is always recommended to try it out with a minimal viable product. This is a concept that is adhered to in lean management, where a product or service is developed with the minimal requirement for it to be validated to decide if it is a success.

One such example could be developing a computer application. Not all features and graphics are necessary to do a quick check that will determine if the software could be a success or not. Another example could be developing an electric car. Let's assume you are tasked with a project like this. The minimal viable product could be the skeleton of a car with the electric motor and some core components needed to see if it is workable. Seat covers and interior decoration might not be essential at this testing stage. Likewise, in any new attempt you make, there could be a minimum that is required to test if the product or service is viable and practical. When you focus only on the relevant areas, you may spend a fraction of a time evaluating a new idea to decide if it will work or fail.

Failing fast can save time and costs and also keep the demotivation at a lower level compared to a failure of an event that took a lot of time, investment, and energy.

Furthermore, when failure is not costly and takes only a little time, employees feel freer to come up with new ideas, and they will not be too worried to try things out as they know it may not have any significant impact on the organization.

Using this methodology, many new concepts and ideas can be tried in a significantly shorter time, and employees get used to accepting failure and

5. Team

moving forward without getting stuck on one product. Failure should be acceptable and encouraged as it's the key to newer innovations.

Therefore, as a leader or manager, your duty will be to create a mindset within the employees that a single failure does not define a person's abilities. This will be critical to strengthen their self-confidence.

5.2.4.4.1. How to Fail Fast

Identify the new ideas to be tried and tested	Allocate it to the respective teams/individuals	Start executing the ideas
Keep track of the progress of the execution	Identify potential challenges	Try to find solutions or work-arounds for the problematic areas
Identify the areas that work well	Document the challenges which were not foreseen	Try the overall success rates of the idea
If the idea is not meeting expectations, drop it	Analyze the reasons for the failure and decide what could have done better	Apply the lessons, retry the idea, and measure the success rates
Avoid teams getting discouraged on failures	Always try the minimal viable product first	If the idea is a total failure, end it permanently
Fail fast to keep the costs and efforts lower	Gain the lessons from the failure	Apply lessons gained when tying something out again

5.2.4.5. Continuous Encouragement

Continuous encouragement is an essential aspect in strengthening the self-confidence of the employees.

Disappointment and feeling guilty for not being able to perform is one factor that disturbs many employees, and sometimes these could even lead to employee resignations. There can be many instances that employees fail individually or as a team. Sometimes they fail with the best efforts, missing success by a small margin.

In all such cases, employees will have an individual disappointment in themselves for not achieving, and teams and team leads will also feel the same. In situations like this, employees will automatically lose some of their self-confidence and may feel they are not capable of any task or are possibly not even worth keeping as an employee.

While failure can be frustrating, as leaders or managers, you need to handle such situations with utmost calm and patience.

Firstly, you need to focus on the reason why the failure occurred. If it was out of the employee's control or was caused by an some unfortunate and unforeseen event, you may need to absorb that pressure for the betterment of everyone else. This is simply because the more you pressure the employees, the worse the situations becomes, and it may not help make the situation better. Therefore, you need to make sure that you always provide encouragement to the individual employees and teams.

You must motivate them throughout to maintain their morale and feel better about themselves. Doing this will create a mindset within employees to give it their best try next time, and they will eventually stretch themselves to the next level so that they do not let the organization and the management down.

Furthermore, as a leader or manager, you need to work on a strategic plan to take the required corrective actions to mitigate risks and the issues pertinent to the previous failures. When the risks are mitigated and the corrective actions are put in place, the employees need to be continuously encouraged and treated with respect and care.

Such practices have proven to allow organizations to be more successful on subsequent attempts, and it has been very successful. The key

5. Team

takeaway from this section is to make sure that you always keep yourself and your employees motivated to navigate turbulent times in your journey toward success.

5.2.4.5.1. How to Improve on Continuous Engagement

Speak to teams positively on their failures	Help them understand that failure is part of the game	Increase the morale of employees
Talk to them about continuous failures that became finally a success	Encourage them by indicating that failure is not the end	Help them understand why they failed
Ask why the teams did not figure it out before	Identify the failure points	Direct the team to try things differently
Give the leadership backing and encourage them to try again	Leadership should always be positive even in failure	Work with the teams to make it a success the next time
Help teams whenever they need your support	Make the teams emotionally strong	Train the teams to never fear failure
Empower teams and upskill if there are any skill gaps	Keep the team momentum at a high level throughout	Learn from mistakes and apply lessons for future use

5.2.5. Career Development

5.2.5.1. Setting the Bigger Picture

Organizations need to make efforts to set the bigger picture for their employees. Sometimes, the employee might be at the beginning of a career. It could even be an intern. However, what is especially important is to set the bigger picture on how an employee could grow within the organization.

Only when this picture is painted will employees feel motivated to put in the effort required to go up on the ladder.

All organizations need to have a clear career plan for any position. Some roles may require a minimum tenure to complete to go to the following levels, and some other roles may require a stretched role that involves managing complex operations and many others. These may vary based on the organization and the nature of operations.

On the other hand, organizations need to have a clear plan and processes to evaluate each employee before they step to the next level. These evaluations are critical as they act as a quality gate for the person to ensure they have what it takes to be successful in their role. Furthermore, organizations need guidance and coaching set up for the employees to take on the journey without significant challenges.

On the other hand, employees who fail multiple times in achieving the bare minimum evaluations cannot move on to the next level. There could be some special cases like this, and organizations need to have clear performance improvement plans that will assist the employees working on the areas they lack.

Sometimes employees may have inherent limitations due to some health challenges. These things need to be carefully evaluated when the reasons for failure are identified. For example, an employee with a hearing challenge may never perform well in a listening test. Therefore, the evaluations need to be based relatively to ensure employees are not evaluated on things they have inherent challenges or limitations on.

As a leader or manager, the key takeaway for you is to ensure you do whatever is needed for employees to grow within your organization and give them a clear picture of what heights they are capable of.

5. Team

5.2.5.1.1. How to Improve on Setting the Big Picture

- Always explain the bigger plan to employees
- Explain the steps to achieving the big plan
- Explain the details of each step and activities
- Help them understand their contribution to the final plan
- Educate them on the organization's end objectives
- Answer questions raised by the employees
- Help them understand why their contributions are important
- Understand how their objectives are aligned with what they wish to do
- Identify their strengths and weaknesses related to the bigger plan
- Assist them on areas where they need support
- Encourage them and explain why you feel they are capable
- Make them feel comfortable being part of the big plan
- Speak to employees continuously to keep track of progress
- Provide timely feedback and solutions when there are roadblocks
- Incorporate valid feedback into the process
- Educate employees to take the same big picture approach
- Don't get frustrated or offended by questions
- Apply the lessons learned for future improvements

5.2.5.2. Career Development Initiatives

Organizations need to take career development initiatives very seriously. While it may appear to be a cost at the beginning, it is an investment. Each employee should have a career development plan based on their role and their capabilities. Some of the career development aspects could be generic ones, while the others could be more job-specific ones.

One main reason for organizations to be reluctant to do this is that employees may leave for better opportunities once they have been trained. This puts the organization in a difficult situation to recover the investment made on a given employee.

When organizations avoid career developments for this reason, there could be another challenge where they will end up with underdeveloped employees. Therefore, organizations need to come up with a win-win model for both them and the employee.

Some thoughts on these areas are for organizations to develop career development initiatives that work on a revenue share basis where the organization pays the employee a revenue share for the skill they bring in.

A simple example is an ISO certification. For an organization to bid for such projects, they need to have certified people within their employee pool. However, certifying employees may need some investment. But if the employee leaves soon after completing the training and certification that the organization sponsored, then the organization will be in a difficult situation to recover the costs associated. A revenue share is a model where the organization provides revenue on a project basis for the employee, motivating him to stay afterwards.

Another model could be signing a bond; however, this has proven ineffective as employees may stay to complete the bond while they may not have a passion for working with an organization.

Another way could be organizations charging a portion from the employee's payroll and then reimbursing it over time. This will eventually allow the organization to recover its investment.

The key takeaway from this section is that employers need to have a comprehensive career development plan for the employees, and the

5. Team

required investments need to be made to mitigate the risk of losing the return on the investments made.

5.2.5.2.1. How to Improve on Career Development Initiatives

Identify the qualification gaps employees have	List in order of priority how these can be achieved	Explain to employees why they need to upskill
Have a budget allocation for career development initiatives	Compare your skillsets with the competition	Understand the overall skill gap areas that exist in the market
Prioritize the immediate skill sets needed for survival	Ensure the teams are upskilled on a timely manner	Plan a model for how the investment could be recovered soon
Have various models to share cost and benefit between employee and organization	Have a career growth and a clear path defined within organization	Explain to employees what they need to do to go to the next level
Recognize and Reward employees who are doing well	Tie KPIs and incentives to career development goals	Take corrective actions on employees who fail to achieve these
Make continuous investments on career development	Leadership should lead by example	Use the lessons learned for future improvements

5.2.5.3. Job Shadowing

Job shadowing is one methodology that organizations can use to support employees in advancing in their careers.

This involves an employee or a group of employees being put together with a senior or more experienced employee to observe how they do a specific task or complete a specific job. Job shadowing can bring a more realistic perspective of how a job operates on the ground, and it could also give more visibility on the real challenges faced on a given job. It is always good for organizations to make job shadowing mandatory if an employee is promoted to a more senior role. This will allow them to understand what it is like to be on the job when they take it over. Furthermore, they will see how their seniors tackle different challenges, and it can also help them change their thought process when it comes to problem-solving.

On the other hand, even the organizations will be able to better understand the suitability of the person who is to be promoted to a specific job role and assess the potential areas of improvement that are required.

This is a win-win situation for both the organization and the employee as it helps them synchronize well, which will help to avoid any disappointments or expectations gaps.

Job shadowing periods and intensity may vary from one job to another and from one industry to another. As a leader or manager, you need to ensure that employees are channeled in the correct avenue for job shadowing. Every individual in a given job may vary from their competence and leadership qualities. Whenever a senior or an experienced person is chosen to be shadowed, organizations need to do a thorough study on them to ensure they can give a realistic job experience in shadowing.

If employees are channeled to a person who is not good at performing their job, then the resources who get shadowed by him may not have a more positive and good experience. Therefore, it is very critical to choose the right resources for the shadowing to ensure it helps others gain better clarity, and if not, those who shadow may also inculcate the wrong practices that are followed by the other resource whom they shadowed, and it may not help the objective of career development.

5. Team

5.2.5.3.1. How to Improve on Job Shadowing

Identify candidates to be put on job shadowing	Identify the employees whom they need to be put with	Speak to the candidates for shadowing and explain the purpose
Identify the candidate's willingness to be put on job shadowing	Put a clean plan with outcomes on job shadowing	Deploy the candidates for job shadowing
Conduct continuous reviews to understand how it is progressing	Assess the overall progress of the shadowing outcomes at the end	Recognize the candidates who were successful
Put the successful candidates on the main job to evaluate how they perform	Identify the candidates who did not do well and take correction actions	Identify the gaps of the resources and upskill them
Shuffle across multiple functions and cross-train with shadowing	Assess the value of employees after they gain multiple skills	Promote the right candidates to the right jobs
Allow employees to choose track changes on their jobs	Management to prioritize on job shadowing on a continuous basis	Use the lessons learned for future improvements

5.2.5.4. Flexibility on Career Path Changes

Flexibility on the career paths means employees can change their career paths if they prove they have what it requires for another job role.

Nowadays, many organizations offer their employees the choice of choosing the career path they wish or to change into a career path they like. Offering this flexibility is crucial for organizations to retain their top talents. This is a win-win situation for an organization and the employee too.

It is a fact that many employees may excel in many career paths, and some would prove themselves even better if they were given the option to change their career paths. However, the organization also needs to ensure that such changes do not and hinder its operation. Therefore, organizations need to have a defined methodology to be made use of when it comes to career changes.

Employees need to be aware of the different career paths they can choose and the entry criteria in shifting from one path to another. While some of these change requests could come from the employee, some could also be a suggestion from the management because some employee performs exceptionally in a given task. However, an employee's consent must be obtained before being positioned in a role they did not intend. If they did, they need to be given an extended grace period to prove themselves. A good approach could be to a slow transition to a role, allowing them to learn each aspect while focusing on their primary role.

Good job shadowing could help them achieve their objectives faster and efficiently. If an employee fails to prove themselves in a new role, they should be given a chance to transition back to their original role. While there can be challenges for an organization, it is good to accommodate such changes both ways as it gives an employee the chance to go back to what they were doing and continue it.

This has to stay aligned with the organization's strategies and policies too. The key takeaway from this section is to ensure organizations stay positive toward career changes as it helps retain talent for the benefit of the organization and the employee.

5.2.5.4.1. How to Improve on Flexibility on Career Path Changes

- Speak to employees to understand their skills
- Understand if they are willing to take a new/different role
- Find out if the employees have the right qualifications
- Provide required training to employees to upskill
- Listen to the career aspirations of employees
- Have a structed method for career changes in place
- Run the employees through a comprehensive assessment process
- Allow them to work on a shadowing role for adequate time
- Allow them to work on partial allocation post completion of shadowing
- Encourage employees on their new journey
- Provide them time to adjust and get used to the new roles
- Have continuous conversations to understand any challenges
- Once they settle in, allow them to work on full allocations
- Conduct more interim reviews to ensure things are on track
- Allow employees if they wish to switch back what they did before
- Allow employees to work on a partial model on both roles if they wish to
- Have a clear career path set for any option they choose
- Make use of the lessons learned for future use

5.2.5.5. Identification of Future Leaders

Identification of future leaders means taking steps to groom the next set of leaders who will be taking on critical roles for an organization. While it is quicker to hire talent externally, it is recommended to identify future leaders within the organization. This is because an organization can have talents that are hidden within the organization. However, the identification of such talents may take time and effort.

As a leader or manager, you must keep a close eye on the exceptional performers, and the organization needs to have a framework or a methodology in place to advance the next generation of leaders. Such initiatives need to be taken over a period, and it may also involve significant investments because it involves career developments for the selected employees.

Future leaders could be identified at many levels starting from a most junior level to the most senior level. Some organizations also practice a fast-track program for employees to grow up on the ladder in a lesser duration than the normal tenure.

Organizations need to have a very transparent methodology when it comes to such selections, and the reasons for the selection need to be visible and explainable. This is particularly important because some of these could be easily interpreted as favoritism. Therefore, a precise evaluation criterion should exist for the betterment of everybody. Furthermore, employees need to be given the opportunity to prove themselves eligible for such a program.

While there can be competition within an organization for such positions, one most important aspect that needs to be evaluated is employee attitudes and softer skills. Aspects like teamwork and collaboration etc., are essential for a future leader, and each employee needs to be evaluated by their direct supervisor and colleagues. This is exceptionally critical because even though an employee is proven to have the technical capability for the job, being a leader is not only about the technical capabilities. It has many elements like positive conversation, empathy, team collaboration, team building, etc. Furthermore, it is important to get the employee to self-evaluate on these areas and then check for the gap between the evaluations done by their managers and colleagues as it gives a clearer picture.

5. Team

However, if the self-evaluation has more significant deviation to either manager or peer evaluation, the employee is not very self-aware.

5.2.5.5.1. How to Improve on Identification of Future Leaders

Keep a close eye on the employees with leadership qualities	Assess the right candidates and their skillsets	Speak to the employees and indicate they are part of next gen leaders
Understand their areas of interest	Provide required coaching and groom the next gen leaders	Give them more responsibilities to assess their performance
Provide constant feedback to employees on their progress	Identify the potential areas they find challenging	Have one-on-one discussions and provide coaching continuously
Provide required emotional support for the future leaders	Put them to work closely with leadership for a period of time	Provide feedback on areas of improvements by leadership
Empower them with the right tools and technologies	Provide them a team to work with	Obtain feedback from the team of their leadership style
Keep their morale up with continuous encouragement	Recognize and reward the best performing ones	Use the lessons learned for future improvements

5.2.5.6. Internal Promotions

Internally promoting people for different roles is something that many organizations have different views on. While some organizations think it's a good idea, others feel it's not so good because when external hires are done, they will walk in with different experiences and knowledge of different markets and customers. Furthermore, their contacts may be different from someone within the organization, and they may be able to help expand a company's network. On the other hand, internal promotions can be helpful as they allow the people who have proven themselves to go up the ladder.

If you look at it from a holistic perspective, while some roles may require external talent, there could be many that may not require such talents where it could be easily fulfilled by an employee who is within the organization.

Internal promotion is a clear indication of the career development and growth of a person within an organization. When people have less room for internal growth, it simply slows down the right talent coming in for a given organization. Therefore, we highly recommend that organizations fulfill all potential and possible roles within the organization as it improves the faith employees have in their organization. Furthermore, it is much easier as these employees are already aware of the organizational dynamics and practices, hence, it will not require any additional time for them to adapt to the organization.

Furthermore, as these employees have proven themselves within, there is no better evaluation criteria to assess them on, where when someone comes in from an external hire, they may or may not adapt well to the organization's dynamics and practice, and furthermore, they may or may not deliver what is expected.

However, there is no more straightforward way to evaluate an external candidate unless an opportunity is given. However, if they do not deliver the desired outcomes, it will be too late to take corrective actions. This would not typically occur if the employee is promoted internally as he or she had already proven themselves, and they will take less time to adapt.

A key takeaway for the leaders and managers is that, for any role that can go with internal promotion, it is always recommended to take that approach first before going into external recruitment as external recruitment

5. Team

may have some elements that need time to get exposed, and this only happens when the real action begins post-hiring.

5.2.5.6.1. How to Improve on Internal Promotions

Prioritize internal candidates first for the new positions available	Be clear on the skills needed for the new roles	Have a clear career path defined for the new role
Identify the potential candidates who are suitable for the new role	Be clear on the strengths and weakness of the identified candidates	Speak to candidates to understand their preference for the role given
Provide the required trainings for the identified candidates	Give required shadowing needed for the role if possible	Have one-on-one conversations to be clear on any challenging areas
Provide required coaching for the right candidates	Provide required emotional support to the candidates	Give them time to be comfortable with their roles
Put the users on the job role on a partial allocation for them to pick things up	Once they are comfortable, put them on full-time	Have continuous follow-up until they feel comfortable
Continuously encourage them on their achievements	Give them continuous support as long as they need	Use the lessons learned for future improvements

5.2.6. Recognition

5.2.6.1. Formal and Informal Recognition

Employee recognition plays an especially important role in employee retention and maintaining employee happiness. There are various types of recognition that organizations could put into practice.

Formal recognition is one such type of recognition where employees are recognized for their efforts. Such recognition is done in a more formal manner, recognizing them at a company awards ceremony or something similar.

Organizations need to have clear guidelines and policies in place for formal recognition. These conditions and guidelines need to be clearly articulated to all employees, and as a leader or manager, it will be your duty to ensure you increase the awareness among your employees.

Formal recognitions are important event, and many organizations do them a minimum of once a year. They can also be done on a smaller scale to keep up employee momentum.

On the other hand, employee recognition can also be done in a more informal way. For informal recognitions, there is no rule book. These can be done at a team level to recognize something important within a team or of a given employee or a group.

When it comes to informal recognition, even a standing ovation to a team member who has helped everyone could be sufficient.

While formal recognitions are done at a lower frequency, informal recognitions can be done more frequently within the teams. Such recognition could help improve employee satisfaction levels, and it could also help organizations get the best output from their employees.

Such activities keep the team engagement levels high, allowing each employee to feel good about themselves, and they will be more cooperative and helpful to each other in achieving similar successes even in the future.

Therefore, as leaders or managers, you need to help to keep the recognitions aspects continuing in the organization as a whole and within the individual teams and also be aware of any achievements by the team members for better clarity and understanding.

5. Team

5.2.6.1.1. How to Improve on Formal and Informal Recognitions

- Focus on both formal and informal recognitions
- Keep the information recognition more often
- Speak to teams often and appreciate them for the good work they do
- Throw small surprise parties to recognize a good effort by someone or a team
- Encourage top levels to follow the same process
- Have ad-hoc quick meetings to share good news
- Appreciate teams whenever possible
- Keep casual conversations with the teams most of the times
- Allocate budgets for the informal recognition
- Leadership needs to get involved in the appreciation
- Know employees by name and speak to them regularly
- Maintain a close relationship with employees
- Add some informal recognition to formal if they are continuous
- Educate teams on the impact of recognitions
- Focus on adding more areas of recognitions to formal recognition
- Obtain employee feedback on recognition
- Incorporate valid and good feedback to the process
- Use the lessons learned for future improvements

5.2.6.2. Special Effort Recognition

Special effort recognitions are a little unique in comparison to the general recognition an organization would have. Such special effort recognitions could be a one-time thing or something that happens as a very exceptional condition.

Some examples of such situations could be an employee going the extra mile to help a customer or an employee risking their job to bring up a critical problem.

Such incidents may vary from one organization to another as well.

What is essential to understand is that any situation that does not usually fit into the standard formal or informal recognition but requires recognition, it will be a special effort recognition. Special effort recognitions could be recognized either formally or informally as well.

While some recognitions could be addressed at an organizational award ceremony, some could also be recognized at a weekly team meeting. It can vary on the impact and how sizable the recognition is. However, the most critical aspect for a leader or manager is to make sure that such incidents never go unrecognized. Some organizations even maintain a unique register book or a memorial notice board that has fellow employees' special contributions.

The most critical part of special recognition is the publicity that is being given to it. Special efforts should be publicized and used to draw the attention of others.

Therefore, as a leader or manager, you need to be aware of what could ideally be a special recognition by understanding what could potentially qualify for such recognition. Furthermore, you need to be able to decide if that goes into formal recognition or a more informal one.

You will also need to decide if the recognition deserves a financial incentive, a token of appreciation, or a thank you note, or a speech. However, it is good to maintain uniformity when it comes to recognitions to make sure employees do not get offended that they are not being recognized in the same way that someone else was.

A comprehensive recognition model will be helpful for organizations to carry out the evaluations in a fair and equal manner for the right

5. Team

employees to be recognized for the efforts they put together for the betterment of the organization.

5.2.6.2.1. How to Improve on Special Effort Recognition

Identify the qualification criteria for special efforts	List all past special recognitions made	Allocate a budget for the special recognition
Speak with the leadership peers to help define criteria	Classify the categories and type of recognition to be given	Have a formal appreciation for such employees or teams
Explain to them what the special recognitions means to the organization	Add the details on a organization notice board	Give tokens of appreciation (i.e. plaque) in addition to gifts
Consider giving a score when it comes to promotions	Create a special recognition organization magazine each year	Share the employee's story to encourage others
Make sure the recognitions are uniform to keep the standards	Analyze if this leads to an increasing trend of employees going an extra mile	Encourage employees to always go an extra mile to help customers
Keep this practice continuously to keep encouraging the teams	Leadership should give prominence to special recognitions	Use the lessons learned for future improvements

5.2.6.3. Comprehensive Scoring

Comprehensive scoring means having a detailed scoring model that captures all the efforts an employee or a team put together at different phases of their career.

Such scoring models must be well thought through to make sure they capture different contributions employees make and assign clear scores to quantify them. Innovativeness, creativeness, and thinking out of the box are some areas these scoring models need to give a broader focus on.

Many traditional scoring models contain a general scoring model that helps capture the employees' standard chores. This is the basis to have. However, with the change in the organizations and market trends, additional elements must be incorporated within these. Furthermore, there are instances where employees extend their support on some notable contributions toward the organizations. Such could be very much different from the standard job function they perform. Employees at times may contribute to greater causes that are not part of the organization, such as taking part in providing voluntary service for some society or a state body or a special group with a greater purpose. When it comes to employee scoring for recognition, organizations need to incorporate these elements to make it a balanced score that captures the job elements and the other elements that are valuable in a more comprehensive manner.

Furthermore, aspects such as employee attitude, helpfulness to fellow employees, positive outlook, and tenure of service are other elements that will help evaluate the employee in a more holistic way. Willingness to upskill is also one such important area. Many employees in organizations get stuck in their comfort zones, where they will put less interest in upskilling themselves on areas essential for their career and which are essential for an organization and its growth. Upskilling should be an area employees are encouraged in as it directly impacts the organization and the outputs. Upskilled employees make an organization resilient and future-proof. Therefore, organizations need to recognize them, but they also need to be supported in a manner that will help them pursue their upskilling journey in a more meaningful way. Furthermore, extending financial support will be an excellent avenue to explore.

5. Team

A key takeaway from this section for leaders and managers is that recognitions should be comprehensive, and they need to be seen from a holistic point of view and not only from a work target standpoint.

5.2.6.3.1. How to Improve on Comprehensive Scoring

Analyze the shortcomings of the current scoring methods	Speak to employees to get their views on the shortcomings	Collect all key parameters needed for comprehensive scoring
Speak to the experts on coming up with a comprehensive scoring method	Show the scoring to the employees and obtain their feedback on improvements	Analyze the practicality of achieving the scores defined
Explain the guidelines to employees clearly	Ensure the scoring process is clear with no ambiguities	Run the soring model to see if it captures all elements
Review captured scoring and run through feedback for improvements	Invest in a solution to capture instant feedback	Avoid last-minute mess-ups that negate past good work
Analyze employee satisfaction of received scores	Keep improving the scoring method over time	Leadership also should be evaluated on the same scoring method
Recognize the best performers	Support employees in their journey to become good scorers	Use the lessons learned for future improvements

5.2.6.4. Increasing Employee Visibility

Increasing employee visibility means giving them visibility to the external world as representatives of the organization. While this can be achieved in different ways, the following are some examples.

Some organizations have yearbooks that get circulated each year that contain slots for employees who have done well. They also have coverage about each department, what they do, and how they contribute to the organization's growth.

Having an employee overview page on the company website is yet another way an organization could help improve employee visibility. Such things vary by organizational size and scale too. Such initiatives need to be scalable where they must cover the complete employee base.

Organizations also need to have initiated employees to encourage them to be on a featured page or a listing in an employee yearbook. Some thoughts around this would be to have competitions or events within an organization that qualify employees to be on a featured page in an article or a popular magazine.

Corporate social media has a great role to play in portraying the employees to the outer world. Organizations can do a weekly or a daily posting about some of their employees and their contributions to the organization. Some articles could contain quotations from the employees. Such campaigns could target holidays, seasons, or other events.

Such awareness is a form of recognition where employees feel good about themselves, and it can also help organizations improve their employee loyalty.

Organizations could also highlight their employees when they excel in some examination, certification, or recognize them for volunteer service. An organization needs to have a dedicated team who will work on these and ensure they are done in a timely manner. These are very important for an organization to portray themselves to the outer world as it has a real impact on the external outlook people have on an organization.

5. Team

5.2.6.4.1. How to Improve on Increasing Employee Visibility

Identify the areas with lack of visibility	Speak to employees to understand which areas have less visibility	Identify the root cause of lack of visibility
Obtain ideas from employees how they wish to increase their visibility	Understand what the competition is doing	Create social media pages if not available
If social media pages are available, increase engagement	Continuously keep posting via social media channels	Come up with programs like employee of the month, etc.
Invest in social media and press to speak about employee achievements	Start an organization yearbook to increase visibility of employees	Have a page on website to speak about employees
Invest in organizational branding	Sponsor events with organizational branding	Promote employee achievements wherever possible
Create employee testimony videos and publish on social media	Sponsor employees for key events that increase visibility	Use lessons learned for future improvements

5.2.6.5. Personal Touch

A personal touch is another important aspect when it comes to employee recognition. Employees naturally feel good about getting recognized by their employer. However, it can be even more impactful if the recognition is personal to each employee.

Personalized gifts directly addressed to an employee by name could mean a lot more than a generic note of appreciation. Furthermore, as leaders or managers, you should always try to address employees by their names. This will give a personal touch and will have a direct impact on employee happiness. Leaders knowing an employee's achievement will make the employees feel better, and they will try to do things even better going forward.

While it can be quite challenging for leaders to remember all employees by name, at least have the department heads brief the leaders on special achievements and recognitions that employees are being given. Leaders and managers should be positive in their communications with the employees, and employees should feel included. Giving attention to the employees is one important aspect that will create a great positive impact.

This is also one way of recognition where employees feel good about being recognized by their leaders. Such attention and recognitions could be extended to a manager meets an employee outside work. This will make a stronger bond between the employee and the leader.

Last but not least, leaders and managers should also consider taking part in the employees' successes and times of sorrow. In the event of a loss of a family member or a calamity, it is recommended that leadership pay a visit to the employee who is affected to indicate to them that they are not alone. These are some simple gestures or recognition that could have lasting impacts on an employee, and this would also help them improve their loyalty to the organization.

5. Team

5.2.6.5.1. How to Improve on Personal Touch

- Try to give personalized recognition to employees
- Speak to employees by name
- Maintain a close relationship with employees
- Stay updated about employee achievements
- Have a process to get employee achievements on a continuous basis
- Be familiar with employee skills and strengths
- Leadership should address employees by name
- Give a personal note of appreciation whenever possible
- Make the gifts personalized (i.e. name engraved) if possible
- Try to be inclusive within organizations and employees
- Avoid any favoritism or bias within organizations
- Avoid any potential unintentional discrimination
- Encourage employees to achieve more
- Have lunches and get-togethers with employees
- Create more opportunities to gel with employees
- Create a hierarchy-neutral environment within work floor
- Keep higher engagement levels with employees
- Use lessons learned for future improvements

5.2.6.6. Budget Allocations

Employee recognition can be costly, and organizations need to be sustainable in their recognition initiatives too. Therefore, the organization needs to allocate the required budgets for employee recognition initiatives.

As a leader or manager, you need to ensure that your organization allocates the required budgets for each financial year for employee recognition. When the organization grows over some time, employee targets and benchmarks should also grow. Therefore, organizations need to ensure their recognition scope also grows to stay on par with its growth.

There can be situations where the organizations need to run cost-cutting initiatives. Turbulent times demand strict measures. However, employee recognition is an area that should be considered only when there are no other options for cost reductions. This is simply because all employees work toward achieving their goals and they want to be recognized. However, when they know there is no recognition anymore, it may simply demotivate them.

When this happens, it could lead organizations to more devastating situations as employee demotivation means a lesser outcome.

Organizations drive cost-saving initiatives as they lack profitability or due to some unfavorable market conditions. Cost-cutting can have various impacts on employees. Cuts in the recognition budgets may demotivate employees further, as they now do not see a reason to stay motivated. This could lead to a situation where the demotivation levels double and eventually lead to deficient performance levels within organizations.

Therefore, the key takeaway for leaders and managers is that the recognition budget is something you need to touch only as the last option for cost-cutting initiatives. It is highly recommended to keep the funding available for employee recognitions at any time as this will be the hidden force behind greater outputs.

Furthermore, all recognition initiatives need to be sustainable for organizations. Therefore, careful evaluation needs to be done before the launch of any recognition schemes as reversing it could be more damaging.

As a leader or manager, you have to ensure that you take necessary steps for sustainable recognition programs and continue their operations even during challenging times.

5.2.6.6.1. How to Improve on Budget Allocations

- Analyze the budgets allocated for recognition
- Identify the shortages within allocations
- Identify the actual requirements of budgets
- Speak with leadership and obtain the required budget allocated
- Ensure the budgets are sustainable
- Find revenue streams which are self-funding
- Avoid cuts on any allocated budgets
- Speak to employees and obtain their feedback on shortcomings
- Try to sustain the quality of rewards given
- Avoid compromising on budgets for rewards due to other external conditions
- Try to be creative in recognition
- Try to obtain scale-based discounts on larger purchase of materials as gifts etc.
- Have an employee contribution toward a fund if needed
- Leadership should contribute toward such funds
- Try to be more innovative in rewards and recognition to create wow factor
- If budgets are a constraint, postpone an event, but never cancel it
- Educate employees the importance organization puts on recognitions
- Use lessons learned for future improvements

www.ingramcontent.com/pod-product-compliance
Lightning Source LLC
Chambersburg PA
CBHW031837170526
45157CB00001B/330